D1543921

Technology, Education—Connections
The TEC Series

The
COMPUTER
CLUBHOUSE

Constructionism and Creativity in Youth Communities

Edited by

Yasmin B. Kafai
Kylie A. Peppler
Robbin N. Chapman

Forewords by

Barton J. Hirsch
Rosalind Hudnell

Teachers College, Columbia University
New York and London

Published by Teachers College Press, 1234 Amsterdam Avenue, New York, NY 10027

Scratch is a project of the Lifelong Kindergarten group at the MIT Media Lab. The Scratch logo and the Scratch cat are trademarks of MIT.

Portions of Chapter 1 previously appeared in Donald A. Schön, Bish Sanyal, and William J. Mitchell (Eds.), *High Technology and Low-Income Communities*. Cambridge: MIT Press. Permission granted by MIT Press.

Library of Congress Cataloging-in-Publication Data

The Computer Clubhouse: constructionism and creativity in youth communities / edited by Yasmin B. Kafai, Kylie A. Peppler, Robbin N. Chapman ; foreword by Rosalind Hudnell ; foreword by Barton Hirsch.
    p. cm. — (Technology, education—connections)
    Includes bibliographical references and index.
    ISBN 978-0-8077-4989-0 (pbk.)—ISBN 978-0-8077-4990-6 (hardcover)
1. After school programs. 2. Urban youth—Education. 3. Computer-assisted instruction. 4. Computer Clubhouse. I. Kafai, Yasmin B. II. Peppler, Kylie A. III. Chapman, Robbin N.
LC34.C65 2009
372.133′4—dc22   2009006990

ISBN 978-0-8077-4989-0 (paperback)
ISBN 978-0-8077-4990-6 (hardcover)

Printed on acid-free paper
Manufactured in the United States of America

16   15   14   13   12   11   10   09   8   7   6   5   4   3   2   1

Dedicated to Seymour A. Papert

Contents

PART III: COLLABORATIONS IN THE CLUBHOUSE COMMUNITY

PART IV: SHOWCASES OF COMPUTER CLUBHOUSE SUCCESSES

Foreword

The Computer Clubhouses—and this book—are not just for techies, or at least not techies as we have traditionally thought of them. Sure, the Clubhouses provide a treasure trove of technological goodies. Each offers an array of high-quality equipment and professional-quality software. There are also instruments and studios for creating original music. The overarching emphasis is on encouraging youth creativity, in young people taking on the role of producing rather than merely consuming technology. Begun in Boston in 1993 during the technology and Internet boom, Computer Clubhouses have flourished and there are now more than 100 Clubhouses in 21 countries.

So who else do the Clubhouses attract beyond the traditional techie crowd? In most schools, classes on computer programming are oriented toward math and science, but these Clubhouses are cut from a different cloth. The strong push for youth creativity turns programming into a vehicle for personal expressiveness. Arts such as graphic design and music flourish, multimedia integrations abound, and links to popular culture draw in youth with a broad array of interests. Here is a place where young people—and these are mostly middle and high school youth in low-income communities—can have fun with their friends while developing twenty-first-century skills in computational literacy.

Just as the Clubhouses appeal to a broader group of youth than the usual math and science techie crowd, so too should this book attract the interest of researchers beyond learning scientists. At present, there is an unfortunate divide between learning scientists, who design and study technologically oriented after-school programs, and applied developmental scientists, who focus on positive youth development programs. These Clubhouses could help to bridge that divide. It is difficult to conceive of an after-school setting that would have a greater emphasis on positive youth development. The core principles for the Clubhouses privilege youth creativity, initiative, and leadership. The development of a supportive peer culture is a central concern. Adults and older youth provide mentoring experiences. Youth learn about diversity through an intranet that enables interactions among Clubhouses around the world.

Applied developmentalists can study many of the processes of interest to them but in a different context, one in which youth learn sophisticated technical skills. Frankly, many after-school programs are good at relationships but not so good at program implementation, so it could be eye-opening to examine developmental processes under these circumstances. Of course, developmentalists also can contribute to understanding and improving the Clubhouses through bringing to bear alternative theoretical frameworks and assessment procedures and more rigorous evaluation methodologies.

The Clubhouses are also worth studying from a policy context. Typically, policy in this domain has focused on putting more young people into the pipeline for STEM (science, technology, engineering, mathematics) careers. But the skills learned in the Clubhouses are relevant to a host of other policy concerns as well. Beyond learning computer programming, young people at the Clubhouses learn marketable skills in product design, project management, teamwork, marketing, and communication. In my own evaluation work with an apprenticeship-oriented after-school program, I have human resource professionals conduct mock job interviews with high school students, and I would expect that Clubhouse veterans would knock the socks off those interviewers with their combination of hard and soft job skills. Thus the Clubhouses are well worth the attention of policy makers concerned with workforce development.

This volume does a good job of introducing us to the world of the Computer Clubhouses and the wonderful work that takes place there. It showcases new developments as the Clubhouses confront implementation challenges and seek new ways to maximize their potential. The researchers and practitioners who author the chapters have an array of complementary goals and make use of different strategies. You will not agree with all of their choices or conclusions, but such is the nature of research and development. The chapters in this volume provide the foundation for the next generation of work. Read them, appreciate what has already been accomplished, and consider the exciting possibilities for the future.

—*Barton J. Hirsch*
Northwestern University

The Computer Clubhouse:
The Intel Perspective

In the early 1990s the Internet arrived with the proliferation of broadband connectivity, sparking the creation of high-flying, pioneering companies and generating billions of dollars in commerce from consumers and businesses making their way online. In the background the Digital Divide became an area of increasing focus and concern among prominent politicians, academics, activists, and advocates for the poor and disadvantaged in our communities. They called for closing the gap between the technology haves and have-nots for fear that vast numbers of people with no physical access, resources, or skills to effectively participate in this emerging information society would no doubt be left behind.

Enter Intel Corporation. We joined the fight to close this Digital Divide and to prepare our youth to enter the workforce in the competitive high-tech world of the twenty-first century. We found in the Computer Clubhouse a proven model that could be replicated globally for businesses and educators to collaborate in a community partnership where caring adult mentors educate young people about and provide them with access and exposure to the wonders of technology in after-school community centers. As you will read in this book, the impact of the Computer Clubhouse on underserved youth around the world has been far-reaching, long lasting, and life changing.

When the Intel Foundation invested in the first Computer Clubhouse at the Computer Museum in Boston, Massachusetts, we could hardly have imagined that the Intel Computer Clubhouse Network would expand to over 100 locations in 21 countries, reaching tens of thousands of youth from underserved communities around the world every year. SRI International's Center for Technology in Learning released a study in July 2008 that described the Computer Clubhouse as a place that is "both intellectually and emotionally safe, a highly challenging learning environment that takes into account the home, school, and social worlds members are part of and builds bridges to their futures." And that it is—from the biannual Teen Summit that brings together 300 members to use their technology skills, teamwork, and imaginations to create solutions for issues faced by their communities to the individual and group projects that develop the budding musician or filmmaker, the Computer Clubhouse orients youth to new possibilities. The environment supports them in taking concrete steps toward achieving their academic and professional goals, making plausible options that were previously difficult for them to imagine. For Intel, we're in the business of making what seems impossible very possible through the innovations that we deliver in our microprocessors every single day. That's why we connect so deeply and so richly to the spirit that the Computer Clubhouse promotes in our up-and-coming generations.

In these times of rapid technology change, ongoing globalization, and increasing demand for top talent, the Computer Clubhouse's mission is more critical now than ever. Intel remains firmly committed to the Computer Clubhouse, and we charge the program's leaders to build on the strong foundation and track record of success to rise to the new challenges on the horizon:

- *Evolution.* Now that we've cleared the hurdle of providing access to youth and providing them with basic computer skills and knowledge, we have an amazing opportunity to take that a step farther to develop engineering- and technology-focused programs that promote advanced skills, critical thinking, and problem solving. A prime example is Cricket, MIT's next-generation robotics technology, which creatively integrates art and engineering.
- *Exposure.* In August 2008 the Intel Foundation announced its commitment to increase our support of the Clubhouse-to-College Scholarship Fund, committing more than $600,000 over 5 years toward secondary education. With scholarships ranging from $2,500 to $10,000, the goals are to expose Computer Clubhouse members to educational opportunities and expand the number of them who pursue college degrees.
- *Engagement.* The Computer Clubhouse design model lives and dies with the engagement of mentors who get involved in the educational development of our young people. Whether that's reaching out to new role models or reaching back to Computer Clubhouse alumni, a pipeline of mentors willing to serve is critical for the program's continued success. Take Nancy Douyon, who joined the Computer Clubhouse at the age of 12, went on to attend college with scholarship assistance from Intel, and never forgot where she came from. Nancy volunteered at a Computer Clubhouse as a mentor and role model, and now is pursuing her master of science in information technologies at the University of Michigan. Nancy appreciates the difference the Computer Clubhouse made in her life.

Congratulations to Yasmin Kafai, Kylie Peppler, and Robbin Chapman on editing this book. Intel is proud to be the sponsor of the Computer Clubhouse and we are looking for you to continue to accomplish great things. In the words of Intel cofounder Robert Noyce, "Don't be encumbered by past history. Go off and do something wonderful." And the Computer Clubhouse is wonderful!

—Rosalind Hudnell
Director of Diversity
Intel Corporation

Acknowledgments

We wish to thank you, the reader, for taking the time to learn more about how innovative after-school learning environments like the Computer Clubhouse can support youth learning and creativity. The extraordinary fact about the Computer Clubhouse model, both in theory and practice, is that it speaks to the ways in which humans of all ages learn, grow, and contribute to their communities. The Computer Clubhouse provides a context where learners can gain fluency with digital technologies and with thinking about their own learning and creativity. A Clubhouse serves as a home for its members, mentors, and coordinators, whether it is situated in Illinois, Ireland, or India. Whatever the lessons that you, the reader, take away from the stories contained here, we hope they will factor into how you think about and build learning environments that empower youth to learn and grow in similar ways.

We also want to applaud all the various people, organizations, and funders involved in making the Computer Clubhouses across the network a creative outlet where learning and creativity are a shared core value. What Clubhouses world-wide have accomplished for their members, and what we have been able to sub-sequently report in this book, would have been impossible without the contributions, both large and small, that have supported the Clubhouse Network over the years. Indeed, it does take a village to raise a Clubhouse. Early support from the Computer Museum, Boys and Girls Clubs, Boston Museum of Science, and other host organizations laid the groundwork for proving the potential of the Clubhouse model to transform the lives of its members. The Intel Corporation lent its support to move the Clubhouse Network to the next level by funding the establishment of 100 additional Computer Clubhouses worldwide. Intel's commitment to the continued growth of Computer Clubhouses has served as an example of how innovative educational programs can be brought to bear to support the creativity, learning, and innovation of a new generation of learners. The work reported in Chapters 4, 6, 8, and 12 was supported by grants from the UCLA Center for Community Partnerships and the National Science Foundation (NSF-0325828) awarded to Yasmin Kafai in collaboration with Mitchel Resnick's research group at the MIT Media Lab and by a dissertation grant from the Spencer Foundation awarded to Kylie Peppler. The work reported in Chapters 7 and 11 was supported by a predoctoral grant from the Ford Foundation awarded to Robbin Chapman and by funding provided by MIT President Emeritus Paul Gray and the Media Lab.

Next, we want to personally honor and celebrate the Computer Clubhouse Network staff, coordinators, mentors, and most importantly, the members. The staff, coordinators, and mentors have given us the opportunity to deepen our understanding of what it takes to make what often seems like magic happen on a regular basis within their Clubhouses. We want to personally acknowledge the Clubhouse coordinators and Network staff who contributed their voices to our "Perspectives from the Field" chapter and the epilogue: Brenda Abanavas, Jeff Arthur, Lee Betton, Gail Breslow, Patricia Díaz, Karen Ellis, Louise Feeney, Natashka Jones, Lynn Murray, Fred Riedel, Almetris Stanley, Luversa Sullivan, and Suha Al Syouf. We want also to thank the HOV (Hear Our Voices) coordinators, mentors, and girls who shared their learning and leadership lessons in Chapters 7 and 11.

Clubhouse youth worldwide are "voting with their feet" by choosing the Computer Clubhouse as a place to share their creativity, learning, and leadership journeys. We also want to acknowledge how members are, through this network of Clubhouses, able to bring their learning and leadership lessons back into their local communities. The life and vitality of every Computer Clubhouse is born and evolves through the continual personal growth and learning relationships that are part and parcel of Clubhouse membership. Thank you to the membership who exemplify, through the fruits of their Clubhouse experiences, the importance of the Clubhouse in the lives of youth worldwide and remind us that "once a member, always a member."

The Computer Clubhouse: A Place for Youth

Yasmin Kafai, Kylie Peppler, and Robbin Chapman

I decided to come to the Computer Clubhouse to learn all other different things that I didn't know. Now I know a whole bunch about computers and programs like Adobe. I stay about 3 or 4 hours. I work on projects. I like to learn new things and make new projects, I especially love to make Pearls and trace pictures of Bart Simpson. You learn a lot of things about computers, that's the fun part . . . try to make a lot of projects about you and other people . . . . Actually, I'm not really good at solving good problems. I know that I can't 'cause I try and try but still can't. At least I try. . . . I help people at school, when we have a computer and something happens or if something is wrong . . . . [I'm] really, really, really, really good at learning things since coming to the Clubhouse.

—Susan, age 10

Me personally, during school I had nowhere where my skills were useful. This is a place I can actually use my skills, like art and 3-D modeling and painting, drawing. It is a wonderful place to, you know, gather around. In a few words, I find it intellectually stimulating. I learn from everybody and they learn from me.

—Anthony, age 11

When I came to this Clubhouse I didn't know how to do [it] . . . but when I did my first project, I found out programming was for me. This is easy when you have a great imagination and when you put in dedication . . . and for everyone who likes to create and use their imagination for expressing themselves.

—Caro, age 15

This book is about the Computer Clubhouse—the idea and the place—that inspires youth to think about themselves as competent, creative, and critical learners and citizens. These are words we rarely hear mentioned in connection with urban youth who are often perceived as causes for concern rather than empowerment.

But this needn't be. There are many examples that showcase today's youth as engaged and thoughtful contributors to society (Leventhal & Brooks-Gunn, 2003). One such place where this occurs within the context of technology is the Computer Clubhouse, which provides a home for youths' creative interests and their personal and intellectual development. By promoting creative and design activities with technology, the Computer Clubhouse bridges the Digital Divide and provides youth with access to key twenty-first-century learning skills. But more than computer skills are at stake. As the quotes given above of Computer Clubhouse members illustrate, they see themselves empowered to learn and help others, to become members of a community, and to develop a vision for their futures.

During the past decade, more than 2,000 community technology centers have opened in the United States, specifically to provide better access to technology in poor communities (Beamish, 1999; Warschauer, 2004). But most community technology centers support only the most basic computer activities such as word processing, e-mail, and Web browsing (Servon & Nelson, 2002). Similarly, many after-school centers (which, unlike community technology centers, focus exclusively on youth) have begun to introduce computers, but they, too, tend to offer only introductory computer activities and educational games (e.g., Cole, 2006; Hirsch, 2005; Zhao, Mishra, & Girod, 2000). What is new and different about the Computer Clubhouse is the focus on creative uses of technology, where youth are encouraged to work on projects of their own interest, including animations, games, videos, and music with professional-level software tools and support from interested and knowledgeable mentors.

The Clubhouse idea that youth should engage in creative activities with technology drew its inspiration from Seymour Papert's theory of constructionism, which postulated that an individual learns best when making artifacts that can be shared with others and that computers offer privileged ways for children to do so (Papert, 1980; Kafai, 2006). As computers moved out of the laboratory into homes, making technology available was seen as more important than anything else given the widely documented inequities in schools and homes in low-income areas (Sutton, 1991). Yet Mitchel Resnick, Natalie Rusk, and Stina Cooke, the founders of the Computer Clubhouse, argued that "access is not enough," (Resnick & Rusk, 1996a) pointing to a need to focus on developing skills and creative expression with computers. Supported by Papert's ideas, the Clubhouse founders pushed way beyond access toward the need for equitable and creative participation in technology. To be able to participate in the digital culture means more than just knowing how to use computers; you also need to be able to create and contribute your ideas.

Today, we are much more comfortable with the notion of youth as creators and participants in the digital culture. Millions of youth participate in networking sites, games, and virtual worlds. So much of their social life has moved online that participation in the digital public has become an essential part of youth identities and their social lives. Places like the Computer Clubhouse play an important role because they give a creative outlet to youth who find that much of what is important to know and do in the digital culture is not valued in their schools. Inner-city youth perhaps experience this disconnect in more dramatic ways, as they are often perceived as standing on the sidelines of technology culture. Schools that service youth in low-income areas typically have few technological resources and community or curricular connections, leaving young people alienated from the formal education system (Leventhal & Brooks-Gunn, 2003). In addition, with a resurgence of the back-to-basics movement currently underway, youth have few opportunities to creatively or critically develop. Art classes, computer science classes, and any type of liberal arts education have been stripped from the nation's poorest schools. After-school centers like the Computer Clubhouse can serve as an important "middle ground" between home and school, providing a comfortable, supportive, and safe space for youth to explore new ideas and develop new skills that are outside the scope of the current schooling curriculum (Hirsch, 2005). Not only does the Computer Clubhouse make an important contribution in local communities, it also serves as a model for other after-school places with its constructionist philosophy.

THE IDEA: CONSTRUCTIONIST THEORY IN CLUBHOUSE PRACTICE

Constructionism views learning as building relationships between old and new knowledge in interactions with others while creating artifacts of social relevance. Papert (1991) once stated:

> Constructionism—the N Word as opposed to the V word—shares constructivism's connotation to learning as building knowledge structures irrespective of the circumstances of learning. It then adds the idea that this happens especially felicitously in a context where the learner is consciously engaged in constructing a public entity whether it's a sand castle on the beach or a theory of the universe. (p.1)

Several aspects of the Computer Clubhouse embody these ideas of knowledge construction in the design of the activities, materials, space, and pedagogy that constitute the learning culture.

For Papert, artifacts or objects play a central role in the knowledge construction process. He coined the term "objects-to-think-with" as an illustration of how objects in the physical and digital world, such as programs, robots, and games, can become objects in the mind that help to construct, examine, and revise connections between old and new knowledge (Papert, 1980). Playing and interacting with these objects is an important aspect of knowledge construction. The kind of project making promoted in the Computer Clubhouse Network takes on this role of objects-to-think-with, allowing members to engage with technology, problem solving, and artistic expression in profound ways.

An example of what the principles of constructionism look like in action can be found in familiar construction kits like LEGO bricks, Lincoln Logs, or wooden blocks. Papert carried over this type of learning activity into the virtual realm when he designed the Logo software. In the constructionist tradition the Logo software is a form of computational construction kit that allows programmers to design or construct their own software programs to create games, animation, or art. LEGO Mindstorms extend these constructions into the robotics domain, allowing the creation of cars and animated sculptures. Many of these construction kits are found in Computer Clubhouses to provide members with various creative tools to design and implement their own projects. In Chapters 3, 4, and 12, we will describe some new construction kits, such as Scratch, specifically designed in this tradition for the Computer Clubhouse.

Unlike school projects, which might have prescribed procedures and single solutions, Clubhouse artifacts or objects can be developed in an exploratory fashion, at times without a specific end product in mind. Many Clubhouse projects promote an improvised bricoleur-like approach in which a member tinkers around with problems and assesses different solutions until finding an appropriate one. This approach is nothing like a top-down or formal planning approach often favored in the school that sees each step as a smaller stepping stone toward a more advanced construction (Turkle & Papert, 1990). There are also no teachers in the Clubhouse who instruct members about how to complete their projects. This emphasis on learning, and not teaching, often aligns constructionism with discovery learning (Kafai, 2006), which asserts that learning happens as children interact with a carefully considered learning environment without the use of direct instruction. By extension, a common myth associated with constructionism is that any guided instruction is inappropriate for learning. As we found out in our research in Computer Clubhouses, the creation of a design culture requires substantial support and direction from Clubhouse coordinators and mentors, less so in telling Clubhouse members what to do but more so in helping them develop their own ideas.

For that reason, coordinators and/or mentors play important roles of guides, coaches, and colearners who provide Clubhouse members with just-in-time technical expertise or motivational support along the way. The Clubhouse mentor model is a key part of the Computer Clubhouse culture, and handbooks for new mentors often stress these important distinctions between teaching and mentoring (see Chapter 8). These learning relationships that members build with mentors are essential to constructionist learning and the success of the Clubhouse culture (see Chapters 10, 11, and 12).

In many ways, the Clubhouse represents a constructionist learning culture that creates a supportive space for its members to design, build, and share their projects and ideas. Papert always stressed the importance of learning cultures rather than individual activities or tools (Papert, 1980; Zagal & Bruckman, 2005). For him, learning French was best done while being in France; all other means and approaches are poor approximations of not only what it means to speak but also to be French. As such, the Computer Clubhouse creates a technology culture that members can join by speaking the language of technology in creating, building, and sharing their projects—very much like professionals do in their design studios. In the Clubhouse, members are users and creators of technology culture and become immersed in its critical and creative aspects. The idea of creating spaces for youth to have access as well as become technologically fluent ultimately formed the foundation of the first Computer Clubhouse.

THE PLACE: A LOOK INSIDE THE CLUBHOUSE

Beginnings

The first Computer Clubhouse was founded in 1993 by the MIT Media Lab and the Computer Museum. The Clubhouse was started after exhibit designers observed youth sneaking repeatedly into exhibits to spend more time with the toys and tools for making games, robotic designs, or graphic animations. Thus the idea was born to have a space that could be a "creative invention studio" where young members learn by doing, working closely with adult mentors as they explore new ideas, express themselves through their project designs, and increase self-confidence and leadership skills (Resnick, Rusk, & Cooke, 1999). In the following years, several new Computer Clubhouses were established mostly in the Boston area with the support of a variety of corporate, foundation, and individual sponsors. These Clubhouses were based on the original Computer Clubhouse, now called the Flagship Clubhouse, located at the Museum of Science in Boston, Massachusetts. Four guiding principles informed the development of new Clubhouses, providing a lens through which to understand and implement the learning model:

1. Support learning through design experiences;
2. Help members build on their own interests;
3. Cultivate an emergent community of learners; and
4. Create an environment of respect and trust.

In 1999 Intel Corporation announced it would sponsor the opening of 100 new Clubhouses throughout the United States and around the world, using the Clubhouse learning model. Community organizations were chosen to host Computer Clubhouses based on their existing interest in providing technology to youth and their alignment with the guiding constructionist philosophy. Therefore, each Clubhouse is a part of an existing local community organization as well as a part of the worldwide Computer Clubhouse Network with over 100 Clubhouses. These Clubhouses are situated in some of the poorest communities on the globe, and, to better service their community, membership in a Computer Clubhouse is always free.

Two thirds of today's Clubhouses were started with support from Intel and the remaining Clubhouses with support from other companies, government agencies, and individuals. The intent was always that the individual Intel-sponsored Clubhouses would have their host organizations take over fund-raising responsibilities after the initial start-up period. Intel-sponsored Clubhouses started with 4 years of support, with diminishing support from years two to four. More recently, that model has been changed to 2 years of start-up support with a second year of diminishing support. That model has been largely successful. Of course, some host organizations have struggled with fund raising, although they had initially indicated they had the means and intention of taking over fund raising necessary to sustain their Clubhouse. As of today, all Clubhouses—whether established with Intel funding or not—are funded through their own fund-raising efforts. Currently, Intel does not fund individual Clubhouses but rather supports the activities of the Computer Clubhouse Network—including start-up support, professional development for Clubhouse staff, ongoing program assistance, quality assurance, evaluation and assessment, and marketing support.

Location and Design

Across the globe, at least 90% of Clubhouses are located in urban areas; a few are located in rural areas including two on Native American land in the United States. Clubhouses are located in underserved communities of mainly poor, working-class, or immigrant populations. Despite the fact that Clubhouses are located in impoverished areas, all youth who come through the door have access to high-quality equipment, ranging from cutting-edge software to professional desk chairs. Clubhouses possess, on average, 20–25 computers organized in clusters along the walls, with 3–4 computers in each cluster. The cluster design and the fact that youth can easily roll their desk chairs between stations facilitate sharing and collaboration. The software that youth have access to include, but is not limited to, Microsoft Office, Bryce 5, Kai's SuperGoo, Painter 7, RPG Maker, Adobe Photoshop, Scratch, and other video, photography, and sound editing software. Around the room, there is usually a rich assortment of materials in addition to computers, such as digital cameras, microphones, markers, paper, or acoustic instruments. These materials are utilized by the members often in an integrated fashion, that is, building on work created or recorded in one environment and altered in another. There are other objects in the space to inspire youth to build and play, including videogame systems, LEGO building blocks, recycled materials, outdated technologies for youth to disassemble, and various board games. Frequently, Clubhouses also include music studio rooms equipped with musical instruments and professional-quality software for youth to create, record, and edit original music. At most Computer Clubhouses, the computers are networked to a central server, where youth have a personal folder that serves as a digital sketchbook or image archive, as well as a repository for finished work. If a central server is unavailable, youth create personal folders on the desktop in a similar fashion.

Members

Each Clubhouse serves close to 250 youth, most coming from working-class families and disenfranchised communities. One or two full-time coordinators staff each Clubhouse, along with a handful of supporting staff and mentors. As a drop-in program, at any given moment there can be anywhere from 5 to 45 youth in the space who stay between 45 minutes to over 4 hours. Walk into any Computer Clubhouse and you're likely to find groups huddled around a central green table, serving as the common area for youth to work away from the computers with paper, pencils, markers, or electronic parts.

Not all youth come to the Computer Clubhouse to engage in the same activities. There are rappers who can consistently be found in the music studio, gamers who participate in any permissible gaming activity (i.e., Xbox games, board games, and Internet games), animators who can usually be found in the back corner doing stop-action animation shorts, socializers who are present in the studio but drift in and out, Web surfers who frequently enjoy surfing the Internet, artists who choose to create with more traditional visual art materials, and scholars who can be found at the green table working on homework or at the computers doing research for a school project. Most youth participate in multiple groups, at least casually. Although most youth end up becoming designers, animators, or rappers, these groups require time and knowledge of the specific practices to fully partake in these activities. Consequently, most newcomers begin by building on their existing identities as gamers, scholars, surfers, or socializers. Long-term members typically begin embracing the Clubhouse norms of valuing the production over the consumption of technology and begin creating a portfolio of work.

The Network

Over 15 years after its inception, the Clubhouse Network continues to expand as applications to join the network keep pouring in from around the world. The title "Computer Clubhouse" is reserved for those spaces within host organizations who successfully apply for Clubhouse status and agree to adhere to the following requirements:

- Have a dedicated, separate area of at least 1,100 feet for the equipment, furnishings, and Clubhouse staff space
- Assign a full-time coordinator for 40 hours per week
- Enter into a licensing agreement with the Computer Clubhouse Network
- Provide suggested features in the Clubhouse learning environment, including computers in clusters and not in classroom style, a central table as a gathering place, chairs on wheels to encourage collaboration, and exhibit space for youth work
- Adhere to Computer Clubhouse guiding principles
- Serve youth weekdays after school and weekends (a minimum of 20 hours per week)
- Provide opportunities for open-ended exploration during that time (versus classes with a fixed curriculum)
- Provide high-end professional software for creative expression and scientific exploration (versus computer games for entertainment only)
- Ensure youth from underserved communities have access to the program
- Encourage the participation of adult mentors who can serve as role models and support the development of a sense of community
- Participate in the broader Clubhouse community through membership in the Intel Computer Clubhouse Network

What makes the Clubhouse unique from other after-school programs is the focus on youth ownership. Clubhouse members take ownership of the space and their projects. Members determine what projects are of interest to work on and how far to pursue them. Additionally, ownership of the space imbues responsibility for governance of that space. Social rules and norms, when necessary, are developed together with the Clubhouse members and staff. Another unique aspect is the interactions between members and mentors. Mentors are not only present to support members' project work; mentors are also present as learners, who work on their own projects as well. Clubhouse members learn as much about learning and project design strategies as they do about the software tools.

PORTRAITS OF THE SITES

Two particular Clubhouses receive special attention in this book, one in Los Angeles (Chapters 3, 7, and 11) and the other in Boston (Chapters 1, 4, 6, and 10), and serve as extended case studies. We delve into the specific programs, outcomes, and case studies at these two sites, providing insight into the particulars of their operations. From 2003 to 2008, Yasmin Kafai, Kylie Peppler, and others in this volume engaged in participant ethnographic research as mentors and researchers at the Youth Opportunities Unlimited (Y.O.U.) Inc. Computer Clubhouse in South Los Angeles, California. This particular Clubhouse is situated in a storefront location in one of the city's poorest areas and equally serves over 1,000 high-poverty African American and Latino youth, many of whom are bilingual. At this Clubhouse, members range in age from 8 to 18, but most are between the ages of 10–14 and come from working-class families. About 45% of members are female. The three Clubhouse coordinators are leading members of the South Los Angeles community and had a prior relationship with the host organization. The majority of the mentors assisting in this Clubhouse are from outside the community, introduced through field experience requirements associated with an education course taught at the University of California at Los Angeles. This Clubhouse was of interest to us as a test site for expanding the repertoire of youths' media manipulation to include programming practices. Proof of a programming culture taking root at this site was recorded between fall 2004 and winter 2006; a closer look at youths' work in this area is presented in later chapters.

From 2002 to 2006, Robbin Chapman and colleagues from the MIT Media Lab were involved in conducting ethnographic research and workshops at the Flagship Computer Clubhouse located in Boston, Massachusetts. Housed in the Museum of Science, it is attended every week by about 250 youth ages 10–18 years old. Over 40% of members are female and Flagship Clubhouse members are from predominantly poor and working-class families. A full-time Clubhouse coordinator, who has been in that role for over a decade, is on staff. A part-time coordinator who is also a member of the Clubhouse Network staff attends on Girls' Day, every Monday. Clubhouse mentors are primarily university students and professionals from various industries, including technology, arts, and business. One of the research projects examined how Clubhouse youth engage in critical reflection, articulate their design work, and how this impacts learning relationships with their peers. The technology development and research approaches and findings are presented in later chapters.

At the same time, this book attempts to paint a picture of the entire network—admittedly, an almost impossible task. The remaining chapters in this book focus on other Clubhouses sprinkled across the globe and provide insights into the on-line network of Clubhouse members and mentors. A table is provided here that summarizes information for each of the featured Clubhouse sites for further refer-ence and comparison (see Table I.1). Each Clubhouse in the network is unique, and naturally there are many that could not be featured here due to space limitations. By focusing in on a few specific sites, we are able to give some depth into certain Clubhouse sites and in the final section, "Showcasing Successes," we are able to give the reader a better sense of the breadth of the network.

THE BROADENING IMPACT OF THE NETWORK

The growing, worldwide network of Computer Clubhouses has continued to find ways to deepen the learning experiences of its members by developing programs to address their needs. Programs that focus on encouraging girls to use technology, on career and college preparation, and on coordinator professional development have all come out of lessons learned about supporting the various needs of those at the Clubhouse. As more Clubhouses were added to the network, it became vital to connect these members across the network through Teen Summits, coordinator retreats, and an online community to ensure that a sense of community is pre-served across the network. As of 2008 the Clubhouse Network had hosted four Teen Summits, serving over 800 Clubhouse members from 20 countries. During the weeklong summits, members work together on projects that address their vari-ous communities' challenges. They also get to network with local engineers, musi-cians, writers, scientists, programmers, animators, and artists. The goals of these programs are to encourage members to see a more expansive, productive future than they may have imagined before joining the Clubhouse.

Professional development of Clubhouse coordinators is an equally vital factor in providing a learning environment that supports creative learning through de-sign activities. As new Clubhouses continue to come online and new coordinators are trained, it becomes even more critical to provide a space where professionals from all Clubhouses can connect. The Computer Clubhouse Annual Conference brings together over 100 Clubhouse staff from around the world to share lessons learned, develop strategies to better support the Clubhouse learning model, and plan for the continued growth of the network. More localized regional workshops take place to keep up the momentum generated at the conference and institute strategies in ways that are relevant to a particular region. Regional coordinators travel between the sites, offering professional development and regular assistance to individual Clubhouses.

A need to connect Clubhouse members, mentors, and coordinators from across the network fueled development of a private intranet, called the Clubhouse Village, where projects and creative ideas can be shared. The Village is an online portal designed to augment the learning experiences of Clubhouse members by connecting them to members from other neighborhoods, cities, and countries, which value the guiding principles of Clubhouse learning. The Village features so-cial networking and communication tools and virtual project galleries, and hosts network-wide learning events and activities. At the time of publication, there were

TABLE I.1. Computer Clubhouse Sites Featured in This Book

Featured Clubhouse	Clubhouse Location	Local Host Organization	Date Founded	(Total Members) Avg No. of Members	Average Member Ages	Languages	Demographics	Member Socio-economic Status	Referenced Chapter(s)
Amman	Amman, Jordan	Princess Basma Resource Youth Center	2004	(120)	10–16	Arabic, English	Middle Eastern		
Bailey	Falls Church, VA, USA	Fairfax County Department of Community and Recreation Services	2002	(80) 15/day	13–16	English, Amharic, Spanish, Somali	African-American, Middle Eastern, Ethiopian, Somali, Latino	Working class, poor	
Belfast	Belfast, United Kingdom	Springvale Learning Center and Greater Shankil Partnership (site 1); Spectrum Centre (site 2)	2005	(380) 50–65/day	10–17	English	Caucasian	Working class	
Charlestown Boys & Girls Club	Charlestown, MA, USA	Boys and Girls Club of Boston	2001	(70) 20/day	10–16	English, Spanish, Portuguese	African-American, Latino	Working class	5
Flagship	Boston, MA, USA	Museum of Science	1993	(244)	10–18	English/Spanish	African American, Latino, Portuguese, Asian	Working class, poor	1, 4, 6, and 10
Gum Springs	Alexandria, VA, USA	Fairfax County Department of Community and Recreation Services	1998	(67)	13–16	English, Amharic	African American, Ethiopian, Kenyan	Working class, poor	
HCCI	New York, NY, USA	Harlem Congregations for Community Improvement	2002	(150) 25/day	10–15	English	African American	Working class, poor	
James Lee	Falls Church, VA, USA	Fairfax County Department of Community and Recreation Services	2004	(100) 15/day	13–17	English, Amharic, Spanish, Somali	African-American, Middle Eastern, Ethiopian, Somali, Latino	Working class, poor	

TABLE I.1. *(continued)*

Mott	Fairfax, VA, USA	Fairfax County Department of Community and Recreation Services	2004	(199)	12–16	English, Amharic, Spanish, Somali	African American, Middle Eastern, Latino, Ethiopian, Somali	Working class, poor, middle class	
Ramallah	Ramallah, Palestine	Youth Development Association	2003	(90)	12–17	Arabic	Middle Eastern		
Reston	Reston, VA, USA	Fairfax County Department of Community and Recreation Services	2004	(74)	12–17	English, Spanish, Arabic	African American, Middle Eastern, Latino	Working class, poor	
Suba Compartir	Bogotá, Colombia	Fundacion Compartir	2002	(135)	8–16	Spanish	Latino		
Tacoma Computer Clubhouse	Tacoma, WA, USA	Allen Renaissance Inc.	2001	unknown	13–17	English, Spanish	African-American, Latino	Working class, poor, homeless	
Willston	Falls Church, VA, USA	Fairfax County Department of Community and Recreation Services	2003	(94)	13–16	English, Amharic, Spanish,	African American, Middle Eastern, Ethiopian, Somali, Latino	Working class, poor	
WYTEC	Chicago, IL, USA	Westside Youth Technical Entrepreneur Center	2008		10–16	English	African American, Latino	Working class, poor	3
Y.O.U. Inc.	South Los Angeles, CA, USA	Youth Opportunities Unlimited Inc.	2005	(1000) 30–45/day	10–16	English/ Spanish	African American, Latino; 45% female and 55% male	Working class, poor	3, 7, and 11

more than 10,000 members of the Village. What started out with one Clubhouse has now grown into an international community.

OVERVIEW OF THE BOOK

The chapters that follow present the intellectual foundations and inquiry that have emerged from our documentation of the theory and practice of the Clubhouse model, our research investigating the creative work produced at the Clubhouse and the collaborative relationships that occur there, and an evaluation of the impact of these activities. All youth and most mentor names have been replaced by pseudonyms (first name only) throughout the book. All Clubhouse staff, however, have chosen to be identified by name. Actual names of individuals are indicated through the presence of both a first and last name when first introduced and subsequently by their last name.

The first part of the book presents a detailed portrait of the Clubhouse model, highlighting its history, guiding principles, and now global identity from multiple perspectives. Chapter 1, by Natalie Rusk, Mitchel Resnick, and Stina Cooke, begins this conversation with a discussion by the founders of the first Computer Clubhouse, who recount the origins of the Clubhouse and outline the genesis of the four key principles that have become the blueprint for other Clubhouses. In Chapter 2 Patricia Díaz, the knowledge manager of the Clubhouse Network, describes the Clubhouse Village and associated community activities. She uses an international Clubhouse project around Cosmo, a puppet that traveled to Clubhouses around the network, to illustrate how members collaborate across geographical, language, and cultural boundaries. Chapter 3, by Kylie Peppler, Robbin Chapman, and Yasmin Kafai, presents a digest of interviews with community organizers, Network staff, and Clubhouse coordinators from across the globe to illuminate how they define their unique roles and how infrastructure and activities create a support system for the Computer Clubhouse model.

The second part, "Creative Constructions," extends our discussion into the projects created in the Computer Clubhouses. These projects are at the heart of Clubhouse activities and our focus is as much on describing the project activities as the kind of learning that goes on while making them. In Chapter 4 Kylie Peppler and Yasmin Kafai showcase games, art, and animation projects created with Scratch, a media-rich design software specifically developed for the Clubhouse, and illustrate how youth appropriate the new software at multiple levels. Amon Millner continues in Chapter 5 by sharing the work from the Hook-ups initiative, where young people learn about interface design, programming, and science concepts by designing and constructing "Hook-ups," real world objects made from recycled or craft materials that can control games, animations, and other computer programs in Scratch. In Chapter 6 Kylie Peppler and Yasmin Kafai examine dance performances to illustrate how Clubhouse members include local dance practices such as Krumping and Clowning in their media productions. After Chapter 6 we include a collection of color plates that illustrate different Clubhouse spaces, examples of youths' projects specially selected by Network staff for inclusion.

The social context for learning at the Clubhouse is featured in the third part, "Collaborations in the Clubhouse Community." At the Clubhouse, learning happens within a complex social network of members, mentors, and staff. This section begins with how members reflect on their projects and share learning insights. In Chapter 7 Robbin Chapman reports on how members, using software for designing reflective artifacts about their design processes, developed a regular practice of articulating and sharing how they learn and develop creative ideas. In Chapter 8 Yasmin Kafai, Shiv Desai, Kylie Peppler, Grace Chiu, and Jesse Moya describe how Clubhouse mentors participate not just as more knowledgeable peers, but also as facilitators, advisors, observers, and, most importantly, as learners in this process. To provide a more global perspective, Elisabeth Sylvan examines in Chapter 9 how members share work and influence each other's creative processes within the online community called the Clubhouse Village, deepening our understanding of how creative ideas are spread in an online environment where learning happens socially.

We wrap up with findings from three different evaluation efforts in the fourth part, "Showcases of Clubhouse Successes." The Clubhouse organization commissions its own periodic evaluations that capture participation, motivation, and learning of Clubhouse members on a larger scale. In Chapter 10 Gail Breslow, the director of the Computer Clubhouse Network, pulls together key findings from several reports that document participation patterns in Clubhouse visits, the technology experiences of Clubhouse members, and youths' learning benefits over several years. Chapter 11, by Brenda Abanavas and Robbin Chapman, is based on a simple observation that girls came in much lower numbers than boys to visit the Clubhouse. This finding, of course, mirrors the well-documented absence of women and minorities in technology industries. This chapter describes and analyzes the efforts to engage girls in challenging projects with the support of others in order to improve their attitudes toward computers and view computers as relevant to their future. Chapter 12, by Yasmin Kafai, Kylie Peppler, Grace Chiu, John Maloney, Natalie Rusk, and Mitchel Resnick, turns our attention to one particular aspect of technology fluency—namely, programming—that was expected to be present from the beginning but turned out to be mostly absent in Clubhouse activities. They examine various normative, political, and technical aspects that contributed to change in one Computer Clubhouse, among them the introduction of a new programming environment oriented toward media production, the increased amount of mentor support, and a university-community partnership. They conclude with reflections on the Computer Clubhouse learning model and further developments.

With over 100 Clubhouses worldwide, the Computer Clubhouse Network has touched the lives of more than 50,000 young people and has been recognized through awards for its innovative and creative learning model. The Computer Clubhouse Network continues to make a difference in the lives of its members and to serve as a model for developing powerful learning opportunities for young people. Community organizations and individuals across the world have been interested in creating after-school learning environments based on the Clubhouse learning model where young people can enjoy the opportunity to express themselves as designers and leaders, have a voice in their communities, and develop as lifelong learners. This book is a first effort to bring together a collection of writings that document, describe, and analyze the creative work, critical engagement, and social support that characterize the Clubhouse model. Our intent is to share this unique model of learning, which will hopefully inspire others to rethink after-school and in-school learning spaces. Creative uses of and with technology should not be a privilege, but a right for all youth.

PART I

THE COMPUTER CLUBHOUSE MODEL

T HE ORIGINAL COMPUTER CLUBHOUSE started in 1993 in the Computer Museum in Boston, Massachusetts, conceived during the time of technology and Internet boom. A driving force for many initiatives then was the lack of access to technology. The Clubhouse founders took this a step further by claiming that "access is not enough" and proposed a place where urban and minority youth could become fluent in designing with technology. The first chapter includes some of the background stories that led cofounders Natalie Rusk, Mitchel Resnick, and Stina Cooke to the implementation of the first Clubhouse which then became the blueprint for network expansion. The founders describe the four guiding principles that defined the Clubhouse model and reflect how over the years these principles have become embedded in Clubhouse activities.

In Chapter 2 Patricia Díaz, the knowledge manager of the Clubhouse Network, talks about the challenges and opportunities in creating a community in the growing network of Clubhouses. The Village, as the Clubhouse's intranet is called, started way before social networking sites such as MySpace or Facebook became popular among youth around the globe to share common interests in music, media, and culture. The story of Cosmo, a puppet who traveled to different Clubhouses within the network, illustrates how Clubhouse members used the Village and video to stay connected with each other. The Village was created to facilitate the sharing of design and ideas and help cross culture and language boundaries in the network. In addition, the Clubhouse Network has developed annual regional conferences and biannual international summits to facilitate face-to-face meetings between coordinators and members of different Clubhouses.

Finally, Chapter 3 showcases the voices of Clubhouse coordinators, community organizers, and Network administrators—the people who set up and coordinate activities in the Clubhouses and the network. As the proverb goes, it takes a village to raise a child—or run a Clubhouse. Through interviews, the editors gathered their insights about what defines the essence of a Computer Clubhouse and makes it distinct from other community technology centers and after-school programs. Coordinators articulate what they do to engage youth in design projects and how they sustain design cultures in the Clubhouses in addition to assuming many other roles in the community. Each Clubhouse often plays a central role in their respective communities by providing a shelter for youth and a connection to the larger world. The Clubhouse Network has scaled the Computer Clubhouse learning model to international communities, learning in the process which ideas translate easily into other cultures and which ones don't. For example, the mentoring concept, a cornerstone of the Clubhouse learning model, required adaptation as it moved across borders.

All the chapters in this part are meant to provide a fuller description of what a Computer Clubhouse is and how the Clubhouse Network has scaled up to a community of over 100 Computer Clubhouses worldwide. With its unique focus on youth empowerment and creative uses of technologies, the Computer Clubhouse showcases that marginalized youth can be found in the driver's seat when it comes to the design of technologies.

Chapter 1

Origins and Guiding Principles of the Computer Clubhouse

Natalie Rusk, Mitchel Resnick, and Stina Cooke

Technology has changed a great deal in the 15 years since we started the first Computer Clubhouse. At that time, no one was carrying around cell phones. Most people had never heard of the Internet. The most popular Web sites today—such as Google, Yahoo, and YouTube—did not yet exist. Although technologies have changed radically, the motivations and needs that led to starting the Computer Clubhouse program have remained the same and continue to drive the program today. So we find it useful to reflect back on the ideas and issues that sparked us to start the first Clubhouse. In this chapter we tell the story of the origins of the first Computer Clubhouse and then discuss the four core principles that have guided the development of the Clubhouse program since its beginning in 1993.

HOW THE COMPUTER CLUBHOUSE STARTED

The first Computer Clubhouse was created in response to a group of children sneaking into a museum. During school vacation week in December 1989, the Computer Museum in downtown Boston offered a robotic workshop for families, using LEGO-Logo robotics materials borrowed from the MIT Media Lab. Anyone could drop in to participate. On the second day a group of four children showed up, speaking to each other in a combination of English and Spanish. One of the boys in the group, about age 11, picked up a small gray LEGO motor. He was shown how to plug it into a power source to turn it on. The motor began to spin. He called out excitedly for his companions to come see. "Míra, míra! Look at this!" The children started to build a car out of LEGO materials and began to program a computer to control the movements of their car. The children came back to the museum day after day, eager to learn more. After playing with the car for a while, they built and programmed a crane to lift the car. At the end of the week, the robotics workshop was over, and the LEGO-Logo robotics materials were returned to MIT.

The next week, the museum was very quiet. At 3:00 in the afternoon, the doors to the museum's large elevator opened. Inside were the boy and his friends. They

17

asked, "LEGO-Logo?" We explained that we no longer had the materials available. They wandered around the museum trying out the exhibits. However, museum exhibits are typically designed for short-term interaction and do not offer opportunities for open-ended design. The children looked disappointed.

A couple weeks later, a museum administrator sent an e-mail message to the staff, warning them to be on the lookout for a group of kids sneaking into the museum, and to alert security if the children were seen. It turned out that these were the same children who had enthusiastically participated in the weeklong robotics workshop. Now, because they were hanging around the museum, they were beginning to get into trouble with security.

We asked around to see if there were local after-school centers where these children could participate, but there were none in the downtown area. We also investigated what technology-based learning programs were available for youth in the greater Boston area. We found community technology centers that offered children opportunities to play educational games or to take classes on basic computer skills, but no programs that provided opportunities for youth to develop their own creative projects.

The children sneaking into the museum wanted something different. They were eager to try out new technologies. Here was a group of children who wanted to keep coming back to the museum to work on projects that we knew were educationally valuable (Resnick, 2006). They were reaching out, but there was nowhere for them to go.

THE CREATION OF THE COMPUTER CLUBHOUSE MODEL

So we began to explore the possibility of creating a new type of learning center that would address the needs and interests of these and other young people in the area. Our goal was to create a learning space where youth could have access not just to the latest computer technology, but also to people who could inspire and support them as they developed creative projects based on their interests. As we developed our plans, we drew on the latest ideas from educational researchers and practitioners, and on our own experiences working in experimental educational projects. We brought together advisors from university research groups and community youth programs. We also met with local youth and put together a youth advisory board.

Out of these discussions emerged the ideas and plans for the first Computer Clubhouse. Early on, we identified four Guiding Principles for the Computer Clubhouse (Resnick & Rusk, 1996a). We applied these principles to set up the first Computer Clubhouse at the Computer Museum. But the principles have continued to play an important role as the Clubhouse Network expanded to more than 100 sites over the past 15 years.

Principle 1: Support Learning Through Design Experiences

What was the secret to the success of the LEGO-Logo workshop that sparked the idea for the first Computer Clubhouse? A key factor, in our minds, was the

PLATE 1.
A filmmaker works with members in Mexico to help them with their documentary. Volunteer mentors like him inspire members to take their projects to the next level and serve as role models.

PLATE 2.
Members of the Girls' Day program at the Flagship Clubhouse proudly display their work together. The Clubhouse Network makes concerted efforts to stimulate girls' sense of self as well as engagement with science and technology.

PLATE 3.
This 17-year-old member of the Good Friend Mission Clubhouse in Taiwan, didn't intend to make a bird, but as he was learning to use Corel Painter his creation gradually began to look like one. Often the imaginations of Clubhouse members take them places that surprise even them.

PLATE 4.
The music studio is used by the Flagship Clubhouse member in the top picture to compose and mix his own beat. The music studio is a popular feature in all Clubhouses, and often inspires youth to perform in public settings, as the flagship alumni in the bottom picture did at the Clubhouse's 10th anniversary.

PLATE 5.
The Clubhouse green table serves many purposes. It's a place for social interaction as well as group projects. In this scene, teens at the Planetario Clubhouse in Guadalajara, Mexico work together during a Crickets workshop conducted by MIT Media Lab representatives.

PLATE 6.
In 2007, members of the Latin American Clubhouses traveled to other countries in the region to exchange ideas and skills. In the top photo, a member from Costa Rica shows members in Mexico how to create t-shirt designs in Adobe Illustrator. In the bottom photo, the girls display the completed designs transferred onto their shirts.

PLATE 7. Teens crowd the computer to see the latest demonstration by Microsoft at the Clubhouse to Career and College (C2C) Fair at the Museum of Science during the Teen Summit 2008. Every two years the Clubhouse Network invites teen leaders from around the world to spend a week in Boston collectively using their technology skills and their imaginations to help create solutions for issues faced by their communities.

PLATE 8.
This magazine cover was created during a track at the 2008 Teen Summit in Boston. 23 teens from 9 different countries collaborated on a compelling 16-piece glossy worthy of professional publication.

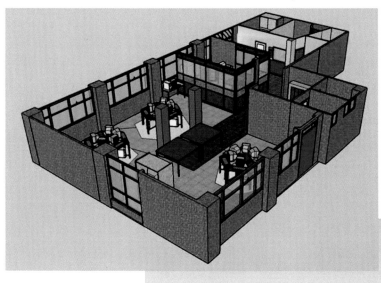

PLATE 9.
Clubhouse members are encouraged to reimagine the world around them both near and far. These two 3D designs inspired by architects represent the work of Clubhouse youth in Bogota and Auckland.

Clubhouse 274

PLATE 10.
For a lot of young people the Clubhouse is the first chance they have to experiment with new tools. At the Clubhouse kids are trusted with expensive cutting-edge technology and encouraged to take their ideas in new directions. By putting themselves in the computer these members at the Haifa Clubhouse become active participants instead of passive consumers of technology.

PLATE 11.
The Computer Clubhouse Network encourages young people to go beyond the four walls of their Clubhouses to express their ideas and opinions. Members from Brazil depicted here participate in a graffiti workshop where they go from sketches on paper to a mural in the neighborhood that showcases themselves.

PLATE 12.
These two youths from Kiryat Gat Clubhouse in Israel (left) and Harland Boys and Girls Club in Atlanta, Georgia (right) experiment with images of themselves, a common Clubhouse activity. Project ideas like photomontages with miniature self-versions are shared through the Village online community and travel quickly across the Clubhouse Network.

PLATE 13.
Some Clubhouse members utilize Clubhouse tools for creative self-expression to develop rich characters and stories. This member from the Bernalillo County Parks and Recreation Clubhouse in New Mexico created a series of Flash animations using unique characters designed by her.

PLATE 14.
Brandy's project "Star Milk."

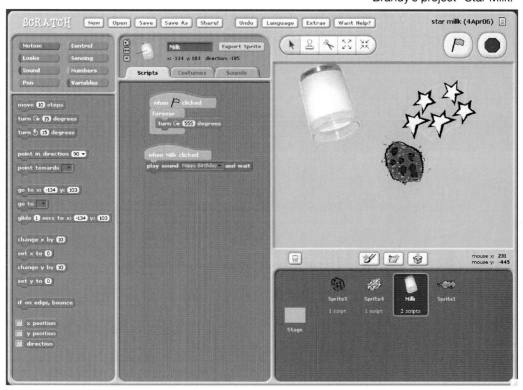

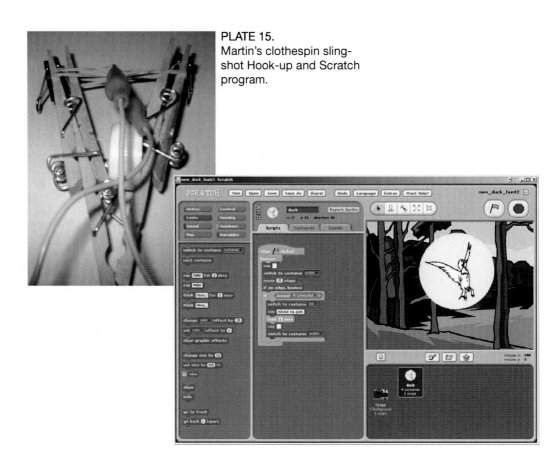

PLATE 15.
Martin's clothespin sling-shot Hook-up and Scratch program.

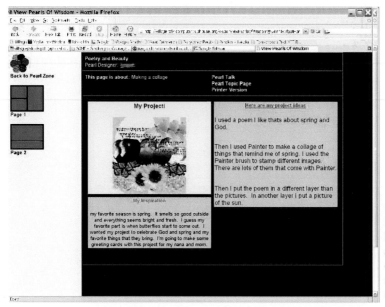

PLATE 16.
Pearl with panel headings, widths, and lengths customized by manipulating the underlying html.

way that participants were actively engaged in designing, creating, and inventing things. Too many educational initiatives try to transmit or deliver information to learners. The Computer Clubhouse is based on a different model of learning and education, where the focus is on *construction* rather than *instruction*.

Indeed, the Clubhouse learning approach draws on an educational philosophy known as *constructionism*, developed by MIT Professor Seymour Papert (1993a). Constructionism is based on two types of construction. First, it asserts that learning is an active process, in which people actively construct knowledge from their experiences in the world. People don't *get* ideas; they *make* them. This aspect of construction comes from the *constructivist* theory of knowledge development by Jean Piaget. To Piaget's concept, Papert added another type of construction, arguing that people construct new knowledge with particular effectiveness when they are engaged in constructing personally meaningful products. Learners might be building a sculpture, writing a poem, composing a song, or programming a computer animation, but what's important is that learners are actively engaged in creating something that is meaningful to themselves or to others around them.

These ideas are at the core of the Clubhouse learning approach. At Clubhouses, young people don't simply interact with technologies, they design and create with technologies. Rather than just watching animations and videos on the Web, Clubhouse members create their own animations and videos. Rather than playing computer games, Clubhouse members create their own computer games (see also Chapter 3).

Activities at Clubhouses vary widely, from constructing robotic inventions to orchestrating virtual dancers to writing lyrics to a song. But these varied activities are all based on a common framework: engaging youth in learning through design. To support these activities, Clubhouses provide a variety of design tools, including tools for digital music recording and editing; Web publishing; computer programming and animation; image and video editing; designing and rendering three-dimensional models, and creating and controlling robotic machines. Clubhouse members often transition quickly from entry-level software to professional-level tools. As Clubhouse members work with these tools, they build toward greater confidence and technical fluency. For example, a young person may start by creating images with a simple paint program like KidPix, then shift to Photoshop to explore more advanced image manipulation and visual effects, then learn to use Scratch or Flash to animate their creations.

At Clubhouses young people not only learn how to use these tools, they learn how to express themselves through these tools. They learn not only the technical details, but also the heuristics of being a good designer: how to conceptualize a project, how to make use of the materials available, how to persist and find alternatives when things go wrong, and how to view a project through the eyes of others. In short, they learn how to manage a complex project from start to finish.

As Clubhouse members work on design projects, they move through what we call the *creative design spiral* (see Figure 1.1). In this process, they imagine what they want to do, create a project based on their ideas, experiment with alternatives, share their ideas and creations with others, and reflect on their experiences—all of which leads them to imagine new ideas and new projects. As youth go through this process, over and over, they learn to develop their own ideas, try them out, test the boundaries, solve problems, get input from others, and generate new ideas based on their experiences.

Young people often begin with a relatively simple design project, such as taking photos of themselves and placing them into a scene. This initial type of project engages them in the creative design spiral over an afternoon or two. For example, they might start by imagining what kind of scene they want to create, then take the photo, edit it into a background (such as a sporting event or favorite place), experiment with visual effects, print and show it to others, and discuss ideas for further projects. After some reflection, they might decide to add more characters to the scene and continue with the next iteration of the spiral.

As young people become more fluent with various tools and aspects of the design process, they often develop bigger plans requiring longer time scales, such as making a stop-motion animation, a sophisticated 3-D model, or a collection of songs for a music album. These projects often become complex and involve more people working together as a team.

Principle 2: Help Members Build on Their Own Interests

In schools of education, the focus is usually on methods of teaching, not motivations for learning. Many courses for educators emphasize how and what to teach, but seldom examine why students might want to learn. When the issue of motivation is addressed, the emphasis is often on extrinsic motivators and incentives, such as grades and prizes based on performance. Why? Many people assume that learning is inherently boring. To motivate students to learn, some educators assume that they need to offer rewards, or turn the subject matter into a competitive game, with prizes for those with the best scores.

If you look outside of school, however, you can find many examples of people learning—in fact, learning exceptionally well—without explicit rewards. Youth who seem to have short attention spans in school often display great concentration on projects that they are truly interested in. They might spend hours learning to play the guitar or perform tricks on a skateboard. Indeed, many of the most successful designers, scientists, and other professionals trace their involvement and success in their fields back to a childhood interest. Clearly, youth interests are a great untapped resource.

When youth care about what they are working on, the dynamic of teaching changes. Rather than being "pushed" to learn, youth work on their own and seek out ideas and advice. Not only are youth more motivated, but they also develop deeper understandings and richer connections to knowledge.

At first, some youth interests might seem to be trivial or shallow, but youth can build up large networks of knowledge related to their interests. Pursuing any topic in depth can lead to connections to other subjects and disciplines. The educational challenge is to find ways to help youth make those connections and develop them more fully. For example, an interest in riding a bicycle can lead to investigations of gearing, the physics of balancing, the evolution of vehicles over time, or the environmental effects of different transportation modes.

Clubhouses are designed to support youth in developing their interests. While youth from high-income households generally have many opportunities to build

FIGURE 1.1. Creative design spiral

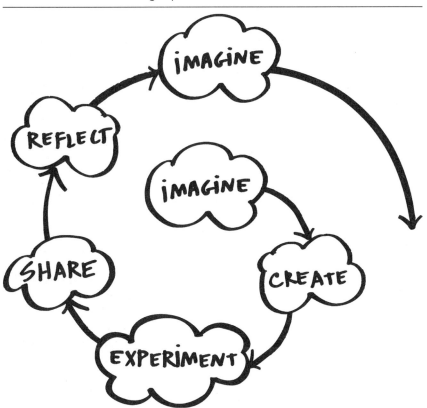

on their interests (for example, music lessons and specialty camps), the youth who typically come to Computer Clubhouses have had few such opportunities. Many have not had the resources and support to identify and explore potential interest areas, let alone to build on them.

Clubhouse participants are encouraged to make their own choices. Just coming to a Clubhouse involves a choice: All of the youth at Clubhouses have chosen to be there, and they can come and go as they please. Once inside a Clubhouse, participants continually confront choices on what to do, how to do it, and whom to work with. Clubhouse staff and mentors help these youth gain experience with self-directed learning, helping them recognize, trust, develop, and deepen their own interests and talents.

Helping youth develop their interests is not just a matter of letting them do what they want. Young people must be given the freedom to follow their fantasies, but they also need the support to make those fantasies come to life. On the walls, shelves, and hard drives of Clubhouses, there are large collections of sample projects, designed to provide participants with a sense of the possible and with multiple entry points for getting started. In one corner of each Clubhouse is a library of books, magazines, and manuals filled with more project ideas (and a sofa to make reading more comfortable). Many youth begin by mimicking a sample project, then work on variations on the theme, and soon develop their own personal path, stemming from their personal interests.

This approach works only if the environment supports a great diversity of possible projects and paths. Young people have a wide variety of different interests, so Clubhouses need to provide a wide variety of different activities to match those interests. The computer plays a key role here. The computer is a type of "universal machine," supporting design projects in many different domains: music, art, science, and mathematics. At any given time, a pair of youth might be using a computer to create a graphic animation, while at the next computer another participant might be using a similar computer to program a robotic construction.

Clubhouse projects often require expertise in a variety of different domains. For example, creating a music video involves recording in the music studio, shooting and editing video, designing an album cover for the CD, and creating a Web site for the group. Such projects allow Clubhouse members with different interests to work together and learn new skills from one another.

Sometimes people misinterpret this guiding principle. When they hear that Clubhouses encourage youth to build on their own interests, they assume that adults need to get out of the way, and let Clubhouse members do everything themselves. For example, we once heard someone propose to lead a workshop for Clubhouse members, helping them learn to create animated comic books. Another person initially dismissed the idea, explaining: "We don't do workshops at the Clubhouse. We let Clubhouse members follow their own interests." But that's not what is intended by this guiding principle. It's important for young people to have choice in what to explore, but they often need a great deal of support in identifying and pursuing their interests. We would advise against a Clubhouse organizing a mandatory workshop where all Clubhouse members were required to learn about animated comic books. But as long as members have the choice of whether or not to participate, we think it's a great idea to offer workshops for Clubhouse members. Such workshops can help Clubhouse members discover what areas they are (or are not) interested in and help them learn new skills that will be useful in pursuing their interests.

Principle 3: Cultivate an Emergent Community of Learners

A typical computer lab for 30 children is set up with 30 computers on tables in straight rows facing the front of the room. This setup is designed for children to face the teacher at the front of the room and to work alone. In contrast, we designed the Clubhouse space with an explicit goal of encouraging and supporting collaboration.

In a typical Computer Clubhouse, each table with a computer has two or three chairs to facilitate youth working together. The tables are placed in small clusters around the edges of room, leaving more space for circulating around the room. The chairs in Clubhouses all have rolling wheels, allowing members to interact with others more easily by rolling over to see what is on another computer. In the middle of each Clubhouse is a large green table without any computers on it. This table acts as a type of village common, where people come together to share ideas and to work on plans, drawings, crafts, and building projects—or simply to have a snack and catch up.

The Clubhouse space is designed to have the feel of a creative design studio, a combination of an art studio, music studio, video studio, and robotics lab. Some of the design choices might seem unimportant (or even extravagant), but we have found that the design of the space deeply influences the attitudes and activities of the participants. As soon as youth walk into the Clubhouse, the setup of the space suggests possibilities. They can see tools and examples to spark their interest and imagination. At one new Computer Clubhouse, the director remarked with surprise that the behavior of the young people changed dramatically for the better when track lighting was installed. And many Clubhouse staff members have noted that the rolling chairs, though sometimes a distraction, make it much easier and more likely for Clubhouse members to share and collaborate with one another.

At Clubhouses, projects are not fixed entities; they grow and evolve over time. Similarly, no one is assigned to work on any particular team, but rather, communities emerge over time. Design teams form informally, coalescing around common interests. Communities are dynamic and flexible, evolving to meet the needs of the project and the interests of the participants (Resnick, 1996).

To support these evolving collaborations, Computer Clubhouses recruit a culturally diverse team of adult mentors—professionals and college students in art, music, science, and technology. Mentors act as coaches, catalysts, and consultants, bringing new project ideas to their Clubhouses. Most mentors volunteer their time (see also Chapter 8). On a typical day there are two or three mentors at a Clubhouse. For example, engineers might be working on robotics projects with Clubhouse participants, artists on graphics and animation projects, programmers on interactive games. For youth who have never interacted with an adult involved in academic or professional careers, this opportunity is pivotal to envisioning themselves following similar career paths.

In this way Clubhouses provide more than just access to technology. Youth in low-income neighborhoods need access not only to new technologies but also to people who know how to use technology in interesting and creative ways. Clubhouses take advantage of an untapped local resource, providing a new way for people in the community to share their skills with local youth.

By involving mentors, Clubhouses provide inner-city youth with a rare opportunity to see adults working on projects. Mentors do not simply provide support or help; many work on their own projects and encourage Clubhouse youth to join in. John Holt (1977) argued that children learn best from adults who are working on things that they themselves care about: "I'm not going to take up painting in the hope that, seeing me, children will get interested in painting. Let people who *already* like to paint, paint where children can see them" (p. 5).

At Clubhouses youth also get a chance to see adults learning. In today's rapidly changing society, perhaps the most important skill of all is the ability to learn new things. It might seem obvious that youth, in order to become good learners, should observe adults learning. But that is rarely the case in schools. Teachers often avoid situations where students will see them learning; they don't want students to see their lack of knowledge. At Clubhouses, youth get to see adults in the act of learning. For some Clubhouse participants it is quite a shock. Several of them were startled one day when a Clubhouse staff member, after debugging a tricky programming problem, exclaimed, "I just learned something!"

For example, two graduate students from a local university decided to start a new robotics project at one of the Boston-area Clubhouses. For several days, they worked on their own; none of the youth seemed particularly interested. But as the project began to take shape, a few youth took notice. One decided to build a new structure to fit on top of the robot, another saw the project as an opportunity to learn about programming. After a month, there was a small team of people working on several robots. Some youth were integrally involved, working on the project every day. Others chipped in from time to time, moving in and out of the project team. The process allowed different youth to contribute to different degrees, at different times—a process that some researchers call *legitimate peripheral participation* (Lave & Wenger, 1991). As youth become more fluent with the technologies at Clubhouses, they too start to act as mentors. Over time, youth begin to take on more mentoring roles, helping introduce newcomers to the equipment, projects, and ideas of the Clubhouse.

Principle 4: Create an Environment of Respect and Trust

When visitors walk into a Clubhouse, they are often impressed by the artistic creations and the technical abilities of Clubhouse participants. But just as often, they are struck by the way Clubhouse youth interact with one another. The Clubhouse approach puts a high priority on developing a culture of respect and trust. These values not only make the Clubhouse an inviting place to spend time, but they are essential for enabling Clubhouse youth to try out new ideas, take risks, follow their interests, and develop fluency with new technologies. Indeed, none of the other guiding principles can be put into practice without an environment of respect and trust.

There are many dimensions to "respect" at Clubhouses: respect for people, respect for ideas, respect for tools and equipment. Mentors and staff set the tone by treating Clubhouse youth with respect. Right from the start, participants are given access to expensive equipment and encouraged to develop their own ideas. "You mean I can use this?" is a common question for youth to ask when they first visit a Clubhouse and find out about the resources and options available to them.

Even with all these options, youth won't take advantage of the opportunities unless they feel "safe" to try out new ideas. In many settings, youth are reluctant to do so, for fear of being judged or even ridiculed. At Clubhouses, the goal is to make participants feel safe to experiment and explore. No one should get criticized for mistakes or "silly" ideas.

Youth are given the time they need to play out their ideas; it is understood that ideas (and people) need time to develop. One new Clubhouse participant spent weeks manipulating a few images over and over. But then, like a toddler who is late in learning to talk but then starts speaking in full sentences, she started using these images to create spectacular graphic animations.

Clubhouse youth are given lots of freedom and choice. One participant explained why he liked the Clubhouse more than school: "There's no one breathing down your neck here." But with this freedom come high standards and high expectations. Clubhouse staff and mentors do not simply dole out praise to improve the self-esteem of the youth. They treat youth more like colleagues, giving them genuine feedback, and pushing them to consider new possibilities. They are always asking: "What could you do next? What other ideas do you have?" Many Clubhouse youth are learning not only new computer skills but new styles of interaction. Clubhouse youth are treated with respect and trust—and they are expected to treat others the same way.

THE EVOLUTION OF THE GUIDING PRINCIPLES

Over the past 15 years these four Guiding Principles have continued to provide a framework of shared values for the expanding network of Computer Clubhouses. But the principles are not static. As new Clubhouses have opened around the world, the Guiding Principles have evolved to fit changing contexts.

When we first talked about "emergent community," for example, we were thinking about the community of staff, mentors, and members within an individual Computer Clubhouse. As time went on, the idea of "community" evolved. Clubhouses began reaching beyond their walls to develop collaborations with their local communities. And as more and more Clubhouses opened, they began to focus on another type of community: the extended community of Clubhouses around the world. Just as new ideas emerge through interactions among members, mentors, and staff within each individual Clubhouse, new ideas also emerge through interactions among the worldwide network of Clubhouses.

The Clubhouse Guiding Principles need not be limited to Clubhouses themselves. In recent years, a growing number of schools and community organizations have expressed interest in the Clubhouse learning approach. One aspect that has received attention is the role of mentors collaborating with youth on creative projects, which differs from the typical one-on-one tutoring in many after-school programs. Hirsch and Wong (2005), in the *Handbook of Youth Mentoring*, describe the Computer Clubhouse approach as a promising direction for mentoring in after-school centers.

A key challenge for the years ahead is to provide support and connections among educators and program staff interested in applying the Clubhouse Guiding Principles in their local settings. With increased access not just to creative applications of technology but also to a dynamic and supportive learning community, more young people around the world will have opportunities to develop as capable, confident, and creative thinkers.

NOTE

Portions of this article previously appeared in Resnick, Rusk, & Cooke, 1999; and Resnick & Rusk, 1996.

Chapter 2

Going Global: Clubhouse Ideas Travel Around the World

Patricia Díaz

Even though the Computer Clubhouse was not created with a vision of global expansion, the Clubhouse model quickly sparked interest nearby as well as abroad and, with the support of Intel, grew into a global network of over 100 Clubhouses in 21 countries over a short period of time. Typically a new Computer Clubhouse opens either in markets where Intel has interests or in communities that have learned about the Clubhouse and are able to gather the resources to support it. This opportunistic nature of expansion has resulted in a widely diverse network, with Clubhouses in Johannesburg, Buenos Aires, Jerusalem, Bangalore, Tucson, Miami, Harlem, and many other places with distinct cultures. The Clubhouse Network makes concerted efforts to connect them and foster collective creations across cultures.

This chapter looks at the opportunities for collaboration brought about by dispersing Clubhouse ideas through the world as influenced both by external factors such as globalization and by internal Clubhouse actions like providing online communities. Through examples of actual projects that have emerged naturally in the network such as regional publications, it describes the possibilities for collective creations that span multiple Clubhouses, with participants who belong to diverse cultures. It highlights the traveling puppet that lasted from June 2005 through February 2007 and was documented through the Clubhouse online community known as the Village.

The traveling puppet, eventually named Cosmo, started as an idea by a mentor in Ireland and became a long-term project that involved many members, mentors, and staff in the Clubhouse Network. In accordance with the Clubhouse philosophy and guiding principles, the traveling puppet built on the common interest of learning about other people's cultures, took advantage of the technology and support infrastructure available in Clubhouses for learning by designing, and was developed in a global environment of respect and trust. Above all, it took to a new level the idea of creating in an emerging community of learners by expanding in time and space beyond typical Clubhouse projects. The traveling puppet is by no means unique in this respect. With the advance of the Internet and the encouragement from the Network staff, creating collectively across cultures is becoming part of the Computer Clubhouse environment as Clubhouse ideas spread around the world.

CONNECTING LIKE-MINDED PEOPLE FROM FAR AWAY

Taking into account that diversity comes in all forms and shapes, fostering a sense of belonging to a single network is not a trivial task. However, there are two strong commonalities that make it possible: the influence of popular media spawned by globalization and the Clubhouse learning model.

Globalization, the growing integration of economies and societies around the world, has effects on all aspects of life that are quite obvious when there are teenagers involved. Adolescents are a prime target for advertisement and in the urban setting similar media conglomerates reach Clubhouse members around the world. Even though this has been happening for a while, recent advances in technology have had a deeper impact in creative processes, providing fertile ground for cross-cultural collaboration in the Clubhouse Network.

This is clear in the Clubhouse music studio, where kids not only listen to similar music but use these as building blocks for their musical creations. Not too long ago, music software was often used to record rhythms and melodies from scratch. Nowadays, software titles that are popular in the clubhouse, like Acid, come with collections of short prerecorded segments—loops—of percussion, bass, keyboards, and many other instruments, that can be easily combined on the screen to provide the rhythmic and harmonic background for rapping. Clubhouse youth then sing or rap on top, often improvising lyrics. This is a relatively new approach to music creation very common in genres like hip-hop, which have spread from New York first to East Asia and Europe and then to the rest of the world. Local elements are often present: The Mexican track may include a mariachi bass guitar while the South African has Zulu words and the Jordanian incorporates Arabic melodies (for another example, see Chapter 6). Yet the overall result and similar practice allow for easy sharing and collaboration, even on a single song, between kids from far away places.

In the arts front Japanese manga and anime are as widespread as hip-hop, providing a model of drawing and animation for youth in places as distant as Chicago, Panama City, or São Paulo. Software like Illustrator, Photoshop, or Painter, and tools such as drawing tablets and scanners, available in the Clubhouses, allow youth to express themselves artistically through the computer (see Figure 2.1).

The theme, language, or subtle artistic choices may reveal the origin of the piece, but the common elements and Japanese influence are much stronger than that. Once again the shared format and field of practice give the youth reasons to start conversations on a virtual forum, ask for advice, or share their artwork as well as their expertise.

Another aspect that all Clubhouses share is the implementation of the Clubhouse learning model, guided and supported by the Network staff based at the

FIGURE 2.1. Drawings by Clubhouse members Travis from Chicago, Bolívar from Panama, and Charlie from Brazil

Museum of Science in Boston and by the Lifelong Kindergarten group at the MIT Media Lab. The learning model influences everything in the Clubhouse from the physical space to the technology available, to the interpersonal relations. Just as they apply to individual Clubhouses, the Guiding Principles (see Chapter 1) have set the tone for interactions across the network. The nonhierarchical structure, in an environment of respect and trust fostered worldwide, has stimulated learning by design with colleagues and peers in faraway Clubhouses.

For example, interest in Internet radio broadcasting from several Clubhouses in Latin America promoted tinkering with various open-source alternatives, brainstorming and problem solving via e-mail and chat, and ultimately designing a radio program that kids in Guadalajara, San Jose, and Bogotá took turns producing week after week, to the delight of listeners in Clubhouses from the United States to Brazil. Listeners in turn had the chance to provide live feedback via chat while the program was being broadcast. The transmissions were modified based on this feedback perpetuating the design cycle. A number of members, mentors, and staff of all ages participated in this learning experience. A similar process was followed in the Asia Pacific region when Clubhouses in Australia, India, New Zealand, the Philippines, and Taiwan decided to collaborate in the production of a regional newsletter.

At the heart of the Clubhouse learning model is the concept of connecting people to their own interests and to other people with intersecting paths in an emerging community of learners. Though stretching these principles to connect with people from other cultures who may speak a different language and live in distant places poses some challenges, it also opens a world of possibilities and increases the chance to find someone with similar interests even if it is just for the sheer number of people to choose from.

Given the influence of popular media described above and the affordances of the technologies available in the Clubhouse, it turns out that kids like Bolívar, a member from Panama who has mastered Illustrator, have more in common with Travis, a member from Chicago who is heavily involved in drawing, than with other youth in Bolívar's own neighborhood. The central support that the Clubhouse Network can provide helps initiate the connection and sustain it over time despite the language and culture barriers.

CONNECTING ONLINE IN THE CLUBHOUSE NETWORK

Tools for long-distance collaboration, such as the Clubhouse intranet Village, are crucial to facilitate collective creations across cultures in the Clubhouse Network (Díaz, 2003). A member describes the potential in the following words: "We have a Web site here called Village and you can include your projects on the Web site so other people can watch them too . . . mostly other Clubhouses, all over the world. It's really cool, you know I can talk to other people in other countries and cities and states that I've never been able to go to; I've been in there in the computer but not in person." The Scratch Web site (Monroy-Hernández & Resnick, 2008) is a public forum where Clubhouse members are encouraged to collaborate with other Clubhouse members as well as worldwide users outside the Clubhouse Network. In 2007–2008, through a collaboration with Tufts University, the network is piloting the use of Zora, a 3-D world that users navigate using avatars (Bers, 2008). Once inside Zora, Clubhouse members can add objects to create and decorate their own structures. They can also link to projects they have uploaded to the Village and showcase them in their three-dimensional space.

Non-Clubhouse tools like Google Earth have also been useful in this context. Announced through the Village and spread via word of mouth, Google Earth was rapidly installed and adopted in Clubhouses from Lakewood, Colorado, to Melbourne, Australia, and many places in between. The initial impetus was to find familiar places and fly to them, but soon enough kids discovered that the free companion software Sketch Up would let them model their own buildings and upload them to Google Earth for others to see. Some Clubhouse replicas are already in the public domain and collaborations are in the works.

CONNECTING IN PERSON AT NETWORK EVENTS

The Clubhouse community does not meet exclusively through virtual channels. Face-to-face interactions of Clubhouse members in the same cluster (i.e., region or close geographic proximity) are encouraged and cherished. Year after year the Clubhouses in Boston hold a cybersummit where kids spend a few days and nights working on collaborative projects with members from other local Clubhouses, culminating in a festive showcase. Clubhouses in New York often meet at LEGO tournaments. In Florida, through government and private grants, there have been mentor sharing and field trips: Every year with the support of Intel, interested Clubhouse members get to travel together on a tour of historical black colleges and universities in the United States.

On a global level, Clubhouse staff meet for professional development at an Annual Conference and regional workshops. Also, every 2 years a group of three youth and a chaperone from each Clubhouse are invited to spend a week in Boston for a Teen Summit. The goal of the summit is to allow youth to meet in person, share ideas, and engage in cross-Clubhouse collaboration. The Teen Summit is designed to encourage members to see their place in the greater network and society at large, and to begin to establish and work toward career and educational goals as well as foster a greater understanding of cultures and youth experiences around the world.

So much is shared that it could be thought of as a Clubhouse culture. In fact, many people affiliated with the network refer to it as "the Clubhouse family." Member Camille describes her first interaction with other members at one of the Clubhouses in the Philippines as follows: "They introduced themselves and they told me that I shouldn't be afraid because 'inside the Clubhouse, we are a family.'" Steve, an alumnus of the Flagship Clubhouse in Boston, says: "I got really into the Clubhouse. I got familiar with the members and mentors, and it was like a big family. My experience there made me more interactive with people. It's not only a great place for learning but for networking with great people while having fun." One way to illustrate how the Computer Clubhouse ideas travel around the world is the Cosmo story described in the next section.

COSMO: A CLUBHOUSE NETWORK STORY

In the midst of the milieu provided by the widely dispersed, culturally diverse Clubhouse Network plus the strong sense of community built on the Clubhouse learning model, many ideas for collective creations across cultures emerge. One of them is what became known to insiders as the traveling puppet. The initial idea came from Dana Wojciechowski, a "traveling mentor" from Basil, Switzerland, while she was spending time at the Foróige Clubhouse in Dublin, Ireland. She proposed to create a creature that could be sent to other Clubhouses to learn about the local culture and travel from one Clubhouse to the next, bringing along locally meaningful souvenirs.

The puppet's purpose was to promote communication between youth from different countries who might not even speak the same language. Kids were to document the process using their favorite media and share it through the online community. They were expected to tell a story together, in the style of urban legends, a modern wayfarer's tale in the form of a short film. With the puppet on a world tour, the kids could go on a virtual journey around the world following the puppet's real trip using the Internet. The bottom line was to create a fun way to foster communication among Clubhouse members from different countries and backgrounds who speak different languages and come from several cultures. Her idea was embraced by the Foróige Clubhouse members who set to the task of sketching and making the puppet from scratch (see Figure 2.2).

Cosmo was born nameless; only through a thoughtful discussion, facilitated by the mentor who conceived the idea, the name Cosmo was chosen. Even though the conversation took place on a public forum on the Internet where others were invited, it was mostly members from the Foróige Clubhouse who participated in this preliminary phase of the project and the discussion was in English. However, one of their considerations when choosing the name was to find a name that would make sense in other languages and other places around the world. Given the purpose of the puppet and the constraints of the community it is hard to think of a better word to describe it. Coming from the Greek *kosmos*, which means uni-

FIGURE 2.2. Initial designs of Cosmo

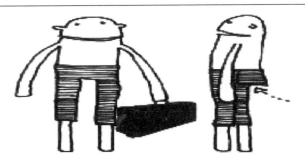

FIGURE 2.3. Excitement at Cosmo's arrival in Colombia

verse, Cosmo sounds familiar in several of the languages spoken at Clubhouses and evokes the image of a cosmopolitan traveler, a citizen of the world.

An amazing quality of the traveling puppet project was its ability to sustain interest among Clubhouse members for very prolonged periods of time. Cosmo was mailed in a box that also carried his belongings. At each stop the box was filled with projects made by the members and, in some cases, local souvenirs or pieces of clothing. The originally tight schedule could not be kept because in some cases international air mail took a while. When Cosmo was shipped from Brazil to Colombia, it got lost in the mail for several months. It took a lot of effort by the Colombian and Brazilian Clubhouse coordinators to recover it. Instead of diminishing the interest, this contributed to the excitement and created momentum that was exploited to the maximum once the puppet arrived (see Figure 2.3).

Taking advantage of the Clubhouse Network online community called the Village, everyone was able to keep track of Cosmo's whereabouts. On the Village there are message boards to post news, an area to upload projects where kids shared photomontages and videos of Cosmo's adventures, and a collaborative section called the Topic Tree where a page was maintained collectively by Cosmo's hosts. This Traveling Puppet page had a gallery that collected all of the projects that the members made with Cosmo; several photo albums with pictures of Cosmo taken by kids around the world; a preview of the posts in the message boards; a slideshow with favorite pictures that kept getting additions as Cosmo circled the globe; and a blog with updates of Cosmo's travels that included embedded videos. Thanks to a tool for online translation incorporated in the Topic Tree and help from volunteer translators, the page was maintained in English and Spanish. Every so often kids would post asking for news of Cosmo or expressing their desire to have him visit their Clubhouse. Here are some samples:

March 10, 2006. Tamarind, member, NM, USA: "That would be awesome, to see Cosmo in person. What a neat project."

March 31, 2006. Jeffrey, member, Philippines: "Come to Clubhouse Philippines (Pilipinas) hope that Cosmo will also come to our clubhouse!!!!!! sana pumunta rin si Cosmo sa aming clubhouse!!!!!!!!!"

April 3, 2006. Lissette, member, FL, USA: "It will be cool to meet Cosmo. It will be very cool to meet Cosmo. I wonder what gifts he would like? What kind of gifts did the other villagers give him?"

April 21, 2006. Gavin, coordinator, Ireland: "Getting Cosmo to your Clubhouse. Hi all . . . I am working on a new timetable for Cosmo's travels. He is currently visiting the Middle East. Watch this space for more."

April 22, 2006. Libby, coordinator, Australia: "I think there are a lot of people who want to see him—he is becoming a cult figure!"

One of the ways in which Cosmo's travels were documented was through videos filmed at each stop (see Chapter 6 for more examples of Clubhouse video productions). The videos were shared through the Village and sent along with Cosmo in the box that carried his luggage and souvenirs from each visit. Cosmo's first video was created in Ireland where the project started. It had music with relevant English lyrics and subtitles, but no dialogue. It had images of Cosmo and kids communicating through body language instead of words. Imagery included a globe, a plane, the Clubhouse in action and pictures of Cosmo next to local and country landmarks. All of these elements were repeated time after time in videos created in other Clubhouses that Cosmo visited, even though there were no explicit guidelines that required them. In a fashion similar to postural and gestural echoing which denote interest for people in close physical proximity without the need for words or a common spoken language, the videos mirrored each other by using similar elements.

The style and story line varied along the way, but the essence was the same. For example, the first plane was a toy airplane moving against a cardboard background and landing on the clubhouse green table. Guadalajara kids used footage of a real plane at the airport showing Cosmo being dropped from the luggage compartment. The Australian movie starts with a clay airplane that flies above the clouds in a carefully placed cinematic sky background before it goes down and shows up as a photograph of a crash.

Pictures next to landmarks were a very important part of Cosmo's journey. In some cases the kids traveled around the city with Cosmo to take the photographs themselves; when landmarks were less accessible they created photomontages. The pictures of Cosmo next to the landmarks were incorporated into the videos and also shared through the Village in a slide show.

Beyond echoing what others had done, Cosmo inspired kids to build on previous adventures, weaving a story together. In Brazil and Mexico, Cosmo met other puppets, frequent visitors of those Clubhouses. In Jordan he met his bride Hamda, designed especially for him, and got married in a traditional Middle Eastern ceremony. While visiting Australia, Cosmo and Hamda had a baby that returned with the couple as a family to Ireland where the journey came to a close. Along the way his interest in music was nourished. Cosmo is seen singing in Dublin, dancing in Guadalajara, recording in Boston, and so on. At times when different hosts met in person, like when Cosmo made an appearance at the Annual Conference or the Teen Summit, the stories were shared and enriched. Central support from Network staff was key to troubleshoot and sustain the momentum through the many months that Cosmo was traveling.

Cosmo sparked interest in visits to far away Clubhouses. In 2007 a small number of members from Latin America traveled with the Clubhouse coordinator to a Clubhouse in a different country in the region to share their expertise, learn from the host and move forward collective projects.

The following quote from Suha, Clubhouse coordinator who hosted Cosmo in Jordan (February 21, 2007), summarizes Cosmo's impact in the Clubhouse Network:

> I remember now the members when they saw Cosmo for the first time, one question on all faces: can't one of us be Cosmo to travel all over the world?!! This was a brilliant idea to inspire the members; I can't wait to see all the project ideas they come up with on the Village and share this wonderful trip with all the members here. Cosmo is proof that it's one Village, and he did it! Even though there were borders between countries! Cosmo crossed the borders and his family is finally safe back home. All of the family members were born and raised in the Computer Clubhouse. Truly we are building a community based on trust and respect from different backgrounds and cultures, following their interest to fulfill their dreams. And "the future belongs to those who believe in the beauty of their dreams"! I hope one day people can travel from place to place making new friends and sharing experiences without fear, war, or anything to stop them. Cosmo is the start, and we hope to have more inspiring projects for the members in the future.

BELONGING TO A GLOBAL COMMUNITY

Big and small things that people take for granted like referring to seasons instead of months stop working when the person at the other end of the conversation enjoys summertime during your winter or does not think of seasons at all. The term *after-school* works well in the United States where kids go to school in the morning but has to be adapted in countries like Costa Rica where *out-of-school* activities take place before some of the schools open in the afternoon. Clubhouses are spread through so many time zones that they are not all in the same day of the week. For part of the day, Clubhouse 274 in New Zealand is literally a day later than most other Clubhouses. As with the flow of the day, there are differences in the flow of the week and the flow the year, many influenced by the different religions, values, and belief systems where some pause for the whole Holy week or the month of Ramadan and some seem to hardly ever stop.

Languages are another issue. People in the Clubhouse Network not only speak different languages but use a variety of character sets and even different writing orientation. There are languages, like Spanish and Portuguese, that are so similar that they give the impression of being interchangeable when they are not, and others, like Russian and Chinese, that are so different that it is hard to find common ground. Staff and mentors that speak more than one language play a crucial role interpreting and translating as do translation tools. Many members use automatic translators online to make sense of e-mails and instant messages received in a language they don't speak. The Village has the interface translated to several languages and a feature that allows volunteer translators to write content of topic pages in alternate languages directly online. Projects that involve audio-visual material help create bridges across languages as did the traveling puppet videos and photomontages.

CONCLUSION

Creating community across cultures cannot be taken for granted. No matter how appealing the idea looked at first sight, the logistics are complex and they bring multiple challenges that need to be addressed in order for cross-Clubhouse projects to blossom. It is possible, and maybe easier, to adopt the Clubhouse learning model locally and keep the collaborations to the immediate community. However, a big part of the motivation to join the network comes from the opportunity to connect kids with others around the world and collaborate with people from far away.

The rewards of belonging to a global community are worth the effort. Kids as well as adults consistently give high marks in internal evaluations to the opportunities to meet, learn from, and collaborate with people from around the world. The Clubhouse learning model has proved to be very conducive to this cross-cultural cooperation. As made clear in the examples discussed in this chapter, though the Guiding Principles were intended for a single Clubhouse, they have been key to facilitating the dispersion of the Clubhouse learning model and creating connections among people around the Clubhouse Network.

Chapter 3

Perspectives from the Field: It Takes a Village to Raise a Clubhouse

Kylie Peppler, Robbin Chapman, and Yasmin Kafai

In this chapter, whose title is inspired by the West African proverb "it takes a village to raise a child," we turn to the people in the Clubhouse Network, the community-based organizations, and the coordinators who run the Clubhouses around the world. While the social, creative, and technological skills employed and learned by Clubhouse members (described in later chapters) are often central to discussions about the benefits of Computer Clubhouses, it is also clear that the coordinators and community organizations at the local level and the Network staff at the organizational level play an equally important part by supporting these endeavors.

We conducted interviews with several Computer Clubhouse coordinators in the United States and abroad, as well as with community leaders and Network administrators (see Table I.1 for a summary of Computer Clubhouse sites featured throughout this book). Our goal was to distill themes of the often intangible aspects involved in supporting and growing the Clubhouse while maintaining its vision. It is impossible to do justice to the numerous aspects that were raised in these conversations so we decided to focus on the following themes: the Computer Clubhouse learning model and what makes it different from other organizations; what it means to be a Clubhouse coordinator in different places around the world; the Clubhouse's role in and contributions to local communities; and how the administration maintains its vision across the Clubhouse Network.

"A COMPUTER CLUBHOUSE IS NOT A COMPUTER LAB"

Gail Breslow, the Network director, put it aptly when she said that Computer Clubhouses are not like any other community technology center or after-school program. Just focusing on the technology alone would be misleading. While technology is key—as the name Computer Clubhouse already implies—technology alone would not be sufficient to realize a successful Clubhouse. So when Brenda Abanavas, a member of the Network staff, noted that "I know instantly when I walk in the door, whether in Atlanta or Belfast, I'm in a Computer Clubhouse," she referred to more than just the presence of a green table and computers. From the outside, Computer Clubhouses share many features of other after-school programs and community technology centers that can be found across the United States and abroad: They have a designated space, they have a coordinator, and they may even have tutors or mentors. But a Clubhouse somehow seems different. The people who have grown and supported successful Clubhouses worldwide offer their insights into the essence of a Clubhouse.

Patricia Díaz, a member of the Network staff, spoke of the adaptability of the learning model being a major factor contributing to Clubhouse success:

> If you want to be [a] Clubhouse, I think it's because you want to embrace the Clubhouse learning model. Now, there are many differences in terms of the actual implementation, but I think those are minor as compared to the essence of the model. So things as trivial as the green table being red in Colombia because green tables weren't standardized when they started—they are still a Computer Clubhouse because they are still learning by designing, they are still a community of learning, and kids explore their own interests. So I think that's way more important and prevalent everywhere in the Network, even if some kids sit on folding chairs and some kids sit on the floor.

Community support prevalent across the Network is driven by partnerships with local, community-based organizations. Host organizations provide the critical link between the needs of a local community and the resources offered by the Network. Host organizations are also responsible for the longevity of their sites, ensuring that funding opportunities and community awareness are communicated to key stakeholders. Many coordinators have voiced how the commitment of their host organization to promoting their Clubhouse is imperative to a successful program. Lee Betton, a community-based organizer responsible for support of six Clubhouses in Fairfax County, Virginia, remarked, "My job is to never be in my office, but to always be at the Clubhouse or in the [executive] offices, or some function talking about the Clubhouse—what they do, and how they [engage] with their local community." These efforts of host organizations translate into increased community support and stronger guarantees that Clubhouses will be a constant resource for youth in their formative years as they develop identities and interests.

Another crucial ingredient to what makes the Clubhouse model unique is the presence of dedicated mentors. Whether adults or other youth, Clubhouse mentors help define the quality of the learning experience for its members. Brenda Abanavas, a member of the Network staff, points to the caliber of volunteers needed at a Clubhouse:

> First of all, I dispel the myth that because you need a volunteer means you take anybody who says that they want to volunteer. It's not true. I feel as though when I have a volunteer that works with me, this has to

be a person who is committed to giving 100+% of themselves, as if they were hired to do that. I look for people who have a mixture of talent and technical skills. I don't necessarily need someone who has years of knowledge in animation, for example, but I want people who'd like to expose themselves to it and to learn enough to excite young people to explore it on their own.

Karen Ellis of the Network staff notes that the Clubhouse Network has invested heavily in mentoring because of its importance to the success of a Clubhouse: "We've created tools like a mentoring toolkit for Clubhouse staff and also for mentors and then created a presence on the Village where our Clubhouses from around the world could talk to each other about mentoring, exchange information and resources, and encourage each other to find mentors.

CLUBHOUSE COORDINATOR: MORE THAN A FULL-TIME JOB

One of the requirements for each Clubhouse is to have a full-time coordinator. As Louise Feeney, the Clubhouse coordinator from Belfast, reports, "The job of a Computer Clubhouse coordinator is just go, go, go! There is so much to do in one day and no one day is the same." Being a Clubhouse coordinator provides her the opportunity to combine her passion for creativity and her interest in education. She says that she is "constantly learning new software and exploring new ideas with young talented thinkers. I have the opportunity to use technology to empower young people." While this is a full-time job in itself, Natashka Jones, the Clubhouse coordinator in Los Angeles, conveys that her position extends beyond the four walls of the Computer Clubhouse by doing such things as going to the schools, checking report cards, and occasionally making visits to the members' homes when they're having trouble at home. She adds, "The role of a coordinator is like a surrogate parent. You become a mentor. You become a best friend. You become a teacher. You become a leader." Other coordinators extend their efforts beyond their official job descriptions in a similar manner. Luversa Sullivan, the Clubhouse coordinator for the Tacoma Clubhouse, recounts that there was a young man at her Clubhouse whose mother had abandoned the family long before. Child Protective Services had taken the young man, making both him and his younger brother wards of the state—moving in and out of different homes, only able to stay 2 months at most, and then moving on to some other home until they found a more permanent situation. Despite the fluctuations in where he slept, ate, and went to school, the young man was able to find familiarity in the Tacoma Clubhouse. Sullivan noted that "the courts thought that this was an important thing for his development. In order to make this happen, the young man and I went with his court-ordered papers in my briefcase. He was frightened and the state knew that there had to be something to give this baby hope or we were going to lose him."

Not only is the Clubhouse Coordinator position vital to the individual success of particular members, the position is essential to the success of the Clubhouse itself. As Karen Ellis conveys, "The success of a Clubhouse is so dependent on the staff, on the connections they can make with their young people and mentors." However, identifying appropriate staff to fill this position can be a challenge. So what do Network staff and community organizers look for during the hiring process? The answer might be somewhat surprising to anyone thinking that it all boils down to in-depth knowledge of information technologies. When asked how best to staff a Clubhouse, Clubhouse practitioners answered, "[Hire] people with a willingness to be open, available, and free with their thoughts. The Clubhouse then becomes a place where doing things, building things, working with youth, and being open to ideas and possibilities result from these kinds of learning relationships. That is how a Clubhouse springs to life." This often means hiring individuals with limited technology expertise but a passion for learning and working with youth. Then Clubhouse Network staff support local Clubhouse coordinators with start-up training about the learning model as well as software applications, ongoing support, online resources on the Village such as a mentoring toolkit and project ideas, site visits and collaborations among local Clubhouse clusters, professional development experiences such as the Annual Conference, regional activities, and—though intended primarily for youth—the Teen Summit, which provides a chance for the entire Clubhouse community to learn from each other. In spite of all this support, it starts with finding the right people for the job.

One of the most important, yet challenging, jobs of any Clubhouse coordinator is to grow and support a culture of design and creativity in the Clubhouse space. While it is a common goal, each coordinator goes about this in a somewhat unique way. For some, the outside mentors and unwavering commitment to the four Guiding Principles of the Clubhouse model largely determine the Clubhouse design culture. For others, peers play a strong role in promoting and developing a design culture. As Suha Al Syouf, the Clubhouse coordinator from the Amman Clubhouse, says, "Let them teach each other, not by forcing, but by guiding them to show others how they could make it better if they work together. The idea of team sprit is very important." Other Clubhouse coordinators take a similar approach. The Tacoma Clubhouse coordinator, Luversa Sullivan, adds her tips for engaging youth who are unfamiliar with the Clubhouse model:

> As youth come into the Clubhouse, they're greeted by other, more experienced Clubhouse members. Most youth at this point are unsure of what they want to do. So the members as well as the coordinator will pose questions, probing the new members for preexisting interests, "Okay, what are you interested in? Are you interested in art? Do you like to draw? Do you like music? Do you like beats?" Once they are able to figure out what they like, the coordinator then views it as her job to show them how the new members' interests connect to other domains, such as taking a drawing and placing a blue screen in back of it to make an animation.

Toward these ends Clubhouse coordinators are unafraid to use popular software, like Harmonix's Rock Band, to capture the youths' initial attention and inspire them to build their own rock bands or videogames in programs like Scratch, a unique visual programming software that was initially created for Clubhouse youth to mix their own media (see Chapter 4).

Engaging youth in the breadth and depth of design activities exposes youth to many different potential career opportunities as well as more general twenty-first-century skills. The Tacoma Clubhouse coordinator remarks, "I think kids will remain engaged as long as everybody continues to make it clear that learning anything takes time. If you do anything over and over again you become a master of it." This type of pedagogical approach is key to the long-term success of Clubhouse youth. Jeff Arthur, one of the Network staff, told us the story of one member with a goal:

> You never know what a member is going to cling onto and then that's going to be their thing. I was asking one of the members heading to college about what she was going to do there and she replied, "Yes, I'm going to be a broadcast journalist." I asked, "OK, how did you find out about that?" She said, "I went to the Teen Summit 2 years ago. At the Teen Summit I was in a track where we went around and interviewed people. Ever since then I knew that that's what I wanted to do for the rest of my life."

THE CLUBHOUSE ROLE IN THE LOCAL COMMUNITY

At the local level, whether in Brooklyn, Johannesburg, or Dublin, Clubhouses have become known to their communities as a refuge and resource for youth. Clubhouse staff is well aware of what their members face every day, both in their schools and in their communities. As Luversa Sullivan observed, "we have a real transient community. A lot of our youth are homeless or their parents are homeless. Some come here from Child Protective Services. But most do things that are meaningful and end up doing something that helps them change their lives."

A community-based organizer for one of the Chicago Clubhouses, Almetris Stanley, described how some of her members "run the gauntlet" just to get to the Clubhouse:

> [A member] created a video about his [everyday] trip to the Clubhouse and what he has to endure to make it to our front door. And he only lives three blocks away. So he has to pass by the drug dealers. They're standing on the corner. Then he is encouraged by the girls pulling on him. They want to take him in another direction. Then he is encountered by some guys shooting dice. But he passes by all of those distractions to get to [our] front door. Once he makes it to the door, he's in a safe haven.

The Clubhouse is a vital part of empowering kids to be productive members of their communities. For example, Clubhouse members in South Africa have created songs about the struggles that they face now in the townships, many addressing the AIDS epidemic. Other Clubhouse members in Johannesburg and Newtown put their Photoshop skills to use in their community by volunteering to design new menus for a local restaurant. Jeff Arthur recalls, "They approached the owner of the restaurant with creating a menu for them with the Photoshop software that they used in the Clubhouse. He ended up using it in the restaurant."

Several Clubhouse coordinators have expressed that Clubhouses provide opportunities for youth from communities that often lack other productive outlets. Suha Al Syouf, Amman Clubhouse coordinator, described what her community would look like without a Clubhouse:

> Without the Clubhouse, my neighborhood would be full of young teen-agers playing in the streets, careless about all the danger, most of the time doing nothing useful for their future. I might see gangs and fights more frequently. Maybe more students dropping out of school. There are some places they can go out to, like a public library and a garden, but it wouldn't provide them with the technology and activities that the Club-house provides. The learning model at the Clubhouse can't be seen any-where else. Youth would be technology illiterate, as their families can't get them computers at home and, if they could, they'd only use it for games. They wouldn't be able to use the software to express themselves and enhance their creative thinking.

Clubhouse adults and members identify and help solve community problems by leveraging the technology skills honed at the Clubhouse. Clubhouse involvement has helped youth at the Tacoma Clubhouse, 70% of whom are homeless, to aspire to higher education. Sullivan proudly says of her members, "I would say 40–45% of our youth go on to college. The other ones get jobs." Similar results are reported across the Clubhouse Network. Almetris Stanley of Chicago shared how her members were learning to start their own company:

> We have a different type of mind-set, I think, because we are really proentrepreneurship. We realized early on that we need a business to help support the not-for-profit part of what we do. So we have started a few businesses and they are still developing. We have a T-shirt business. We had a person to donate everything that we could possibly need for the silk screening and the press. We're trying to get the members to run and use the technology and the space to help not just generate revenue for us but for them. Many members would like to work and they can't find jobs or they're so busy with their schoolwork that they can't work the hours that the job would require. So we're trying to promote a mind-set that not only can you work for a company but you can own the com-pany and set your own hours and still go to college.

In some communities, Clubhouse activities contribute to community efforts to bring disparate parties together and improve the quality of life for youth who must straddle those communities. For example, the Belfast Clubhouse currently exists as two separate physical sites on opposite sides of the Shankill/West Belfast peace line. Decades of war and violence have divided the country. The coordinator, Louise Feeney, shared how members in these two Clubhouse sites worked toward unifying their community:

> Clubhouse members from both communities interact via the Clubhouse Village and Webcam linkups. This is an important first step to breaking barriers and building peace. One multimember project involves collaboration between both Clubhouse sites, and in the process increases both virtual and physical contact between these communities. The Clubhouse is working to increase understanding and to promote reconciliation.

Whatever the local community, the expectation for Clubhouse youth to take responsibility for their projects, their connections, and their community seems to be commonly valued. Coordinator Suha Al Syouf summed it up best with her remark:

> Personally, I feel I'm home if I go anywhere in the world where there is a Clubhouse. We all share the same environment and have the freedom to follow our interest and learn by design. We all speak one language of technology and creativity, no matter what color, name, identity, or religion we are. We all live in one Clubhouse Village, linking us together to share our ideas, projects, and each other.

THE GLOBAL CLUBHOUSE COMMUNITY

The Clubhouse supports members connecting with peers from around the world through its Village Network intranet (see Chapter 9). A coordinator noted, "If you can't travel there by plane, or train, or boat, you can do it on the Village and still be in your Clubhouse community." The Village supports the spread of project ideas and ways to support youth development at the Clubhouses. For example, ideas from South Africa can spread to not only other Clubhouses in the region, but to Clubhouses around the world. Those ideas contribute to improving the work that goes on in the Clubhouses and fostering community. Staffers have noted that the Clubhouse Network is an international organization that manages to be very tight-knit despite thousands of miles between Clubhouses. As Lynn Murray remarked about the Computer Clubhouse Annual Conference, "There's such a kinship among people from across the Network. People are from far-flung areas of the world, together in one room, and quickly become old friends. I think it's the shared value system, the commitment to the mission, and the unwavering agreement among everyone that this is our work that we are committed to doing, and I think it's the tie that binds."

However, making that vision become a reality involved some distinct challenges in maintaining and scaling the original Computer Clubhouse vision. When the Clubhouse Network first started, most of the Computer Clubhouses were based in the United States. Consequently, the network's mentoring resources and materials were focused on needing mentors and defining their role in the Clubhouse model. As Karen Ellis of the Network staff recalls, "It wasn't on our minds to question how is mentoring going to transfer in Ireland, in Brazil, and in South Africa, because at the time, we did not have Clubhouses there."

As the Clubhouse Network grew, the idea around mentoring (or *volunteerism*, as it's now often called) has changed from country to country. In some countries, the word *mentor* just doesn't exist and the ways in which you locate mentors certainly differ as well. To recruit mentors in Boston, you go to a library and put up a volunteer flyer. That makes a lot of sense in Boston but does it make sense in Taipei? Does it make sense in the Clubhouse in Colombia? This presents distinct challenges for Network staff as they craft network-wide resources. In order to make the model successful in other cultures, Network staff turned to Clubhouses to see how they had adopted the mentoring model in order to provide a richer array of options and resources to other Clubhouses. One such solution came in the form of peer mentors or alumni mentors. Ellis recalls, "We looked at Clubhouses in Colombia and in Ireland. In these locations, a lot of their alumni are the mentors. They're actively pursuing that next stage of their role in the Clubhouse: member, then mentor. We weren't seeing that in the United States." This type of challenge cannot always be anticipated during initial conceptualization, but is key to the success of the model as it scales across continents and cultures.

Despite the challenges of being an international network, there are several distinct benefits as well. One of the things most commonly cited by coordinators and Network staff was the access to a worldwide network of like-minded individuals with an array of different talents. Network staff member Brenda Abanavas expressed it this way:

> For me, one of the best things about the Computer Clubhouse Network is the scope of the abilities of the people who are involved. I've never seen the accumulation of such talent in any one place. There are musicians, graphic designers, 3-D designers, IT people, and animators, for example. If you go to the Village and you look at our topic page and you see all the different areas in which someone has an interest in learning some form of technology, there is a whole network of people out there who are highly skilled at those areas.

But Lynn Murray noted that it is not just the resources, it is the culture of sharing:

> The resources and skills across the network—they're so deep and rich. There are so many people in the network with a variety of skill-sets and knowledge, so we are our own resource. And the sharing that's encouraged through the Village—just the exchange of skills and knowledge and support to one another. If you need something, you have all these people, not just the network staff.

CONCLUSION

The Computer Clubhouse model owes its uniqueness to the integration of informal learning and youth development opportunities via creative uses of technology. Youth can develop their projects and make the most of their access to peers, Clubhouse coordinators, mentors, community organizers, and the network—all playing a vital role in making a Computer Clubhouse more than just a computer lab. Upon becoming members, youth are expected to take responsibility for their project activities and roles in the community. They have ownership of a learning environment where they are trusted and respected. This casts the Clubhouse as a youth empowerment program in addition to a technology program and makes the Clubhouse a unique forum for youth to practice learning, creativity, and citizenship by leveraging technologies and learning relationships.

PART II

CREATIVE CONSTRUCTIONS

Becoming a designer, instead of a consumer, of new technologies is a core value of any Computer Clubhouse. Design projects at the Computer Clubhouse take on many different shapes and forms across the network. Yet at every Clubhouse, youth have access to an impressive array of professional and educational software, all of which keep the value of designing at the heart of members' activities. Youth can edit photos in Photoshop, create Web sites in Adobe Dreamweaver, make animations in Flash or Poser, edit video in Premiere, compose original songs in AcidPro, design games in RPG Maker, and make kinetic sculptures or robots with LEGO Mindstorms kits. However, there are several types of software and activities that are uniquely designed for, or created by, those in the Clubhouse space. In this section, we focus on some of these unique efforts to design new software and activities to engage youth in a wide array of twenty-first-century technology practices and highlight the learning that takes place while youth are engaged in these projects.

Kylie Peppler and Yasmin Kafai's chapter in this part presents Scratch, a media-rich visual programming software created specifically to engage Clubhouse youth in media mixing as they learn to program. The authors followed one Clubhouse of early adopters in South Los Angeles and present examples of work collected over the course of a 2-year period, discussing youths' learning of important mathematical and computational ideas while also gaining a deeper understanding of the process of art and design. Their observations suggest that youth leverage previous knowledge in the design process, appropriating design software through personal and epistemological connections to their work.

In the next chapter, Amon Millner describes what is known as the Hookups initiative in the Boston Clubhouses. This chapter highlights both the project and what youth learned by designing and constructing "Hook-ups"—physical objects, like joysticks or a steering wheel, that can control games, animations, or other computer programs in Scratch. In creating Hook-ups from recycled or craft materials, young people work with objects and materials to develop design skills, explore design strategies and learn scientific concepts in the process.

While many youth engage in design projects individually, creating collectively is also a way to bring together members of the community. In the final chapter of this part, Kylie Peppler and Yasmin Kafai describe a unique happening in the Los Angeles Clubhouse community that features youth capturing their collective dance circles. In this project, members of the Clubhouse performed Krump, a new and highly original dance tradition that originated in the South Los Angeles community, and captured their group performances via video documentation. This project describes how the happenings at the Clubhouse are very much influenced by the local context. It also showcases youth leadership skills as members of this Clubhouse entirely conceived of and executed these prolonged projects.

While these chapters are by no means a complete list, the examples and cases presented here give the reader an insider's look at some of the distinctive design projects that have emerged across the network, some of which have already started to extend into schools and other institutions. The findings in this part paint a picture of the complexity and variety of design work that youth engage in at the Clubhouse and provide insights into teaching and learning in the twenty-first century. Learning in this landscape cuts across discipline boundaries, builds on youths' prior interest in new technologies and media, and connects people across cultures, which should arguably be at the heart of any learning institution.

Chapter 4

Making Games, Art, and Animations with Scratch

Kylie Peppler and Yasmin Kafai

A piece of art created in a Clubhouse by an 8-year-old special education student features a picture of a glass of milk, a hand-drawn cookie, and a clip art image of stars that is animated to rotate and change colors at dizzying speeds when the viewer clicks the screen. At the same time, a recording of the artist's loose rendition of Happy Birthday plays. This piece is particularly interesting because the designer is unable to read or write beyond an emergent level but has tied together images, sound, and animation in order to create a personally meaningful and powerfully communicative project using a visual computer programming language called Scratch.

Scratch, a media-rich visual programming software, was created especially for the Computer Clubhouse community to mix new media while simultaneously learning to computer program (Resnick, Kafai, & Maeda, 2003; Maloney et al., 2004). The software is now freely available on the Scratch Web site (www.scratch. mit.edu) and was originally created through a grant from the National Science Foundation awarded to Mitchel Resnick and his Lifelong Kindergarten group at the MIT Media Lab together with Yasmin Kafai and her research team then at the UCLA Graduate School of Education and Information Studies. Mixing a variety of sounds, images, drawings, and photos, Scratch allows youth to easily create their own video games, art, and animations, and then share their creations with others on the Web. Being able to mix a rich assortment of digital media and create interactive work by snapping together building blocks, much like LEGO building blocks, allows youth to take control of the computer in a way that other applications, like Kai's SuperGoo, just doesn't allow. As youth create Scratch projects, they learn important mathematical and computational ideas, while also gaining a deeper understanding of the process of art and design.

Computer programming and media mixing within the context of Scratch can be easy to use and facilitates the creation of digital art. Youth are now able to share creations like this within a Scratch online community, which allows creators from all over the world to view, comment on, download, and remix existing Scratch projects. Our observations suggest that youth leverage previous knowledge in the

design process, appropriating the design software through personal and epistemological connections to their work. While youth were engaging in Scratch, we
found that they were learning a variety of new concepts and knowledge important to professionals in creative, critical, and technical fields. In this chapter, we
illustrate how media mixing led to the eventual widespread adoption of Scratch
within the Clubhouse and beyond through an online community. We followed
one Clubhouse of early adopters in South Los Angeles and present example work
from three cases over a 2-year period, discussing the learning that took place in the
design process as youth appropriated Scratch as a tool for their self-expression.

SCRATCH IN THE CLUBHOUSE COMMUNITY

The success of the new software Scratch was largely dependent on whether and
to what extent youth were able to appropriate it into their cultural, personal, and
epistemological worlds. In other words, ultimately youth needed to make Scratch
a part of their Clubhouse practices while also exhibiting technological fluency and
an acquisition of new knowledge though this process. In constructionism we often talk about the process of appropriation, which posits that learners construct
knowledge by making it their own, as a key aspect of learning (Papert, 1980). In
this chapter, we demonstrate that tools like Scratch or any type of software or
artifact introduced at the Clubhouse can be appropriated by the learner as well.
Papert argued that learners appropriate knowledge through the making of (1) personal connections (i.e., connections to outside interests, past experiences, or prior
knowledge) and (2) epistemological connections (i.e., connections to important
domains of knowledge).

More specifically, we focus on three areas of epistemological connections that
are particularly important to the Clubhouse youths' work in Scratch: connections
to the arts, media, and new technology. These three fields encapsulate the majority
of the connections that we have observed youth making to important domains of
knowledge that would be recognized in professional fields. This type of situated
learning takes place as youth learn the big ideas of computer programming (see
Chapter 11). We summarize this as the technological connections that youth make
in Scratch, which also include learning to debug technology problems when they
arise, as well as becoming more technology fluent. Clubhouse members' design
projects are a natural springboard into learning how computers function, particularly by encountering new technical problems, exposure to computer programming, and various types of logical thinking problems.

These technical experiences take on many shapes in the various projects but
share a common denominator: Youth at the Clubhouse are looking at the computer
in a whole new way—as a new medium for expression and particularly one that
requires them to know how to manipulate features to achieve creative ends, sharing many skill sets with computer scientists and professional media artists (Maeda,
2004). A recent report from the National Academy of Sciences highlights the powerful new domain of Information Technology and Creative Practices (ITCP) in the
arts and design (Lenhart, Madden, & Hitlin, 2005; Mitchell, Inouye, & Blumenthal,
2003; Roberts, Foehr, & Rideout, 2005). The integrated domain of ITCP yields a

variety of culturally significant results, ranging from innovative computer animation, electronic music, and virtual games that are already part of young people's
worlds. In constructing their Scratch projects, youth learn to become more delib-
erate in their artistic choices and, in the process, often draw connections between
several modalities.

In addition to the artistic and technical expertise developed, members use
Scratch as a way to engage critically in the world, fostering their ability to decode
and evaluate popular media designs, understanding references made in popular
designs, and deconstructing and interpreting the meaning behind such designs
(Buckingham, 2003; Peppler & Kafai, 2007). This is somewhat unique especially
for after-school settings and is in large part due to the media-mixing abilities in
Scratch. In our observations, youth naturally pull on their cultural resources as
well as popular media in their work. In this chapter and throughout this book,
we discuss some of the challenges and opportunities for critical engagement in
informal settings.

Taken together, these artistic, media, and technological connections form the
basis for a complex set of contemporary practices, expanding what it means to
be truly fluent in today's multimedia landscape well beyond traditional forms of
print literacy. These expanded forms of literacy are not only important to media
educators, but are of value to a host of other fields, including computer science
and the arts.

A CLOSER LOOK AT SCRATCH

Though Scratch is not the first programming environment aimed at novice programmers (Guzdial, 2003; Kelleher & Pausch, 2005), it is among the first to emphasize media manipulation and programming activities that resonate with the
interests of youth, such as creating animated stories, games, and interactive presen-
tations. In today's media landscape, youth define themselves in relation to popular
culture phenomena in music, video games, sports, Internet, television, and film. In
fact, most youth immerse themselves in several forms of media concurrently in the
after-school hours, often doing homework with their iPods playing, chat screens
going, and television playing in the background. By allowing youth to incorporate
their interests in new media, this becomes a natural springboard into creative production. In fact, youth are significantly more likely to persist in a creative project if
it references popular culture in some way (Peppler & Kafai, 2007).

The Scratch screen (see Figure 4.1) is divided into four areas. On the right is
the stage; a button on the bar below the stage allows the stage to be displayed in
full-screen mode to show off a finished project. Below the stage is an area that
shows thumbnails of all sprites (or onscreen objects) in the project; clicking on one
of these thumbnails selects the corresponding sprite. The middle pane allows the
user to view and change the scripts, costumes (images), or sounds of the selected
sprite. The left pane is the palette of command blocks that can be dragged into the
scripting area; the palette is divided into eight color-coded categories. A Scratch
project consists of a fixed stage (background) and a number of movable sprites, or
onscreen objects. Each object contains its own set of images, sounds, variables, and

FIGURE 4.1. Screenshot of Scratch interface with labels

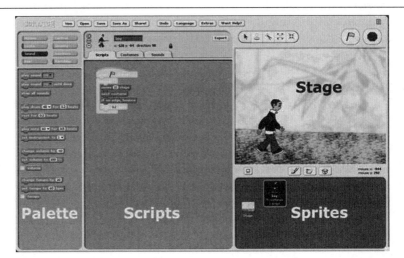

scripts. Visual programming of these objects can be done by dragging command blocks from a palette into the scripting pane and assembling them, like puzzle pieces, to create "stacks" of blocks. This user interface design grew out of a desire to make the key concepts of Scratch as tangible and manifest as possible. Having the command palette visible at all times invites exploration. A user who notices an interesting command can double-click it right in the palette to see what it does. A user can watch stacks in the scripting area highlight as the action unfolds on the stage. These explorations are supported by having the palette, scripting area, and stage simultaneously visible, providing the user with a process model of how their scripts are interpreted by the computer, creating visibility in a world often hidden from the consumer.

MEDIA MIXING WITH SCRATCH

We observed Scratch activities at the South Los Angeles Clubhouse with predominantly Latino and African American youth ages 8–18 and collected all their projects for over a period of 2 years. Clubhouse youth created a variety of projects such as animated stories, video-game art, and interactive or playable art using pop culture images and sounds. Using a comparative case study approach, the youth highlighted in this chapter were selected from over 30 other case study participants based on the prototypical nature of their work and their persistent interest in Scratch over a period of multiple weeks. Each case presents a novel take on how members of the South Los Angeles Clubhouse community appropriated Scratch, as well as highlighting the type of learning that each project exemplifies. Most of these projects are a remix of found images, ideas, and sounds that have been imported into Scratch and uniquely remixed.

Media Art Making with Brandy

"Star Milk," which was presented in the introduction of this chapter, was created by an 8-year-old African American girl named Brandy, who was unable to read or write beyond an emergent level at the time of this study, but was able to create a unique and expressive work of art using Scratch (see Plate 14) (Peppler, 2007). This piece was intended to be a birthday card for the Clubhouse coordinator, and Brandy made connections to her personal and cultural experiences of birthday celebrations, birthday cards, and the birthday song.

Most notably, this piece of art is a good example of the connections that Brandy made to creative or artistic fields, such as media arts. While the term *media arts* is used frequently, it's also used interchangeably with *digital arts* and/or *new media* in many contexts. When a group of professional media artists gathered to discuss the work being produced at the Clubhouse, they were particularly struck by this piece as being exemplary in the collection (Peppler, 2007; Peppler, 2008). Generally, the professional media artists saw this piece as a being successful and "informed by the vocabulary of Scratch." They noted that the quality of the Happy Birthday song was striking because she improvised a new melody around the traditional version, and that the work displayed an unexpected choice of images given the idea for the piece and intrigued the viewer by the interesting coloring scheme and composition. Importantly, the professional media artists compared Brandy's work with that of professional media artists, like Ben Benjamin, and, more generally, blues singers. Clearly, the work being done at the Computer Clubhouse presents opportunities for youth to engage in meaningful and expressive work, which has qualities that can be connected to work being produced in a professional context.

Brandy also made ties to other epistemological domains, such as traditional literacy. In fact, Scratch became a tool for Brandy to reengage in traditional literacies and the schooling curriculum. Ironically, Brandy probably learned to computer program at a novice level before learning to read or write at this same proficiency. In the piece depicted in Plate 14, Brandy used computer-programming concepts like loops and user inputs in this piece. Through working to express herself using a computer language, she was able to make the connection to other types of traditional literacies, which ultimately inspired her to try again at learning to read and write. In Brandy's own words, "Scratch is like a map because it helps me learn"—a powerful testimonial by someone who would otherwise be considered illiterate or preliterate by many.

Music Video Animations with Kaylee

Our second example comes from a 12-year-old African American girl named Kaylee, an avid consumer of pop and R&B music and music videos (Peppler & Kafai, 2007). Frequent activities at the Clubhouse include looking up song lyrics online, singing, and downloading images of her favorite stars. For her first Scratch project, titled "k2b" (see Figure 4.2), Kaylee created a music video based on Gwen Stefani's "Hollaback Girl" (2005). In this sense, the "k2b" project makes several personal connections to Kaylee's outside interests and prior knowledge of popular culture. The Stefani song responds to a disparaging remark by a fellow musician likening Stefani to a popularity-obsessed high school cheerleader. Stefani's track is set in an imaginary high school and relays the message that insults are not things that she tolerates. In the refrain Stefani asserts that she "ain't no Hollaback Girl," referencing backup members of a cheerleading squad whose job it is to holler back the calls of the head cheerleader. A possible interpretation of Stefani's meaning is that she is choosing not to return insults with words but rather responds by stepping it up with an inventive comeback.

"k2b's" likeness to the original video reveals how closely Kaylee studied the original lyrics and music video and yet reinvented it with a spin. Once a user presses the start button, the "Hollaback Girl" track begins and twelve predominantly female avatars dance on screen. Like Stefani's video, these characters are dressed in a variety of costumes and are programmed to perform dance steps often imitating the choreography of the original. The "k2b" video also alternates between urban, school-themed backdrops. Toward the end of Stefani's version, cheerleaders hold up cue cards that spell "B-A-N-A-N-A-S." At the same point in the song in "k2b," Kaylee programs blue and yellow letters, spelling B-A-N-A-N-A-S, to flash and spin on screen. Furthermore, Kaylee becomes a participant in a larger design culture by posting her work for others to view online. On the Village, an intranet for the Computer Clubhouse Network (see Chapter 8), her project has received over 600 hits from members around the world, a sign that she's created a Scratch project that has stimulated a lot of interest. Kaylee quickly learned how difficult it was to choreograph and direct a complex animation.

Undoubtedly, Kaylee is making connections to the traditional arts, media education, and computer science. The aesthetics of the images played an important role in the design process. In the search for "k2b" images, it was less important to her to insert an image of herself than to find one that fitted her perception of how a music video should appear, underscoring the importance of understanding and emulating contemporary art and pop culture aesthetics. Additional connections to traditional arts include the designer's attention to the choreographing of dancers. "k2b" required precise timing and unique dance moves for each of her characters onscreen. Thus Kaylee was making connections to various arts domains and building an understanding of animation, choreography, music videos, and film. During these design moments, programming took a back seat to design considerations of when characters should enter and exit the stage and how each of the dancers should move, which are roles seldom assumed by youth in the traditional arts. Kaylee also made epistemological connections to computer science. This is exemplified by the designer's use of programming concepts like looping constructs, conditionals, and assembling programs out of base components—concepts that are even difficult for novice computer science majors. In addition, she was able to repurpose code in a meaningful way and accomplish artistic design goals for the piece by taking pieces of code and creatively recombining them for new characters.

The elements that Kaylee chose to alter from the original illuminate how she was critically reflecting on the music video. For instance, while Kaylee chose a school setting in "k2b" similar to that in Stefani's video, she had in fact inserted

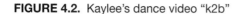

FIGURE 4.2. Kaylee's dance video "k2b"

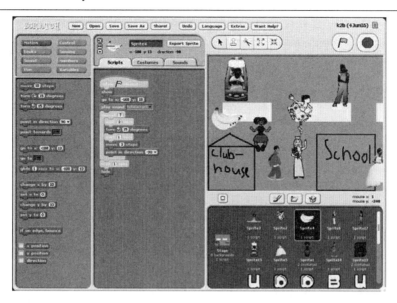

pictures of her own school in Los Angeles, in addition to urban settings that reminded her of her neighborhood (even employing a hand-drawn aerial view of her path between school and the Computer Clubhouse). While the blue and yellow color palette of her work reminds one of the colors featured in Stefani's video, a backdrop of a UCLA tennis court leads one to suspect that Kaylee chose these colors because they are UCLA's school colors, the university that Kaylee hoped to attend. Perhaps most conspicuously, images of Gwen Stefani are nowhere to be found. Kaylee was adamant that she didn't want a picture of Stefani; rather, she wanted a picture of herself and one of her little brother. In the search for these images, Kaylee was very particular about the "look" that she was trying to achieve; her knowledge of pop culture made her very discriminating about the images that she chose, rejecting images of herself in her church clothes because it wouldn't be appropriate for a music video.

What does it mean for a 12-year-old girl to insert herself as the lead singer of this song and why would she want to do this? Because of Kaylee's frequent activity of downloading and studying the lyrics of her favorite songs, one can deduce that she chose "Hollaback Girl" for her video not because she merely liked how it sounded, but because the message of the song was one that she found particularly relevant to her life. Based on discussions with Kaylee about her experiences, this song resonated with her in the way that she navigated—and felt others should navigate—middle school, where often fights break out over petty insults. Furthermore, by placing elements in the video that highlighted her life, her school, and her family, we see the value that she placed in her upbringing. Kaylee's particularity regarding the ways that "k2b" should look like a "real" video demonstrated that the elite world of Kaylee's pop idols was not superior to images of her family and her environs. This demonstrates that Kaylee was making critical connections to popular culture and youth culture themes of power, confrontation, and resistance, which are common among school-age youth fighting to be heard and recognized.

Video Game Making with Jorge

In our last example, we draw from a video game called "Metal Slug Hell Zone X," created by a 15-year-old Latino male designer named Jorge, who modeled the piece after a popular video game with a similar title (Peppler & Kafai, 2007). The original Metal Slug is a futuristic "run and gun video game" widely known for its sense of humor, fluid hand-drawn animation, and fast-paced, two-player action. At home Jorge had a passion for video gaming, and at the Clubhouse he spent the majority of his time working on Scratch projects. "Metal Slug Hell Zone X" was his second project. When the viewer presses a start button, a title screen prompts the player to choose one of four avatars. The selected avatar then appears on the screen in a barren purple desert landscape with moving clouds overhead. Players use the arrow keys to move forward and backward, crouch, jump, and fire a gun (see Figure 4.3). Jorge clearly relied on his personal interests in video gaming as well as his prior knowledge of the Metal Slug games to create this work, which reflect that Jorge was able to forge several strong personal connections to Scratch while making his video game.

Jorge mixed a full range of creative software to make his project. Using the paint editor within Scratch, Jorge paid meticulous attention to realistically animating the avatar as it moved. He made sketches based on playing the original video game, downloaded sample avatars from Internet fan sites, and refined each frame of the movement in the paint editor for smooth stop-action animation. Utilizing the visual programming capabilities of Scratch, Jorge animated these images to respond to keystrokes so that the avatar walks effortlessly across the screen or jumps when prompted by control keys. Jorge used standard design conventions found in video games, even creating special responses if the avatar is told to do something (such as shoot) while crouching or jumping. He learned how to design for interactive play and redesigned his program several times, discovering that it can be friendlier to the user to design a game that responds to standard key strokes (e.g., right and left arrow keys) rather than random characters on the keyboard.

Jorge also learned how to participate in the distributed online culture specific to designing and making fan video games. Scratch facilitated his understanding of how games are made by professional production specialists and he also networked with other fans, like himself, who want to create amateur productions. In this sense, Jorge learned about the art of animation and video-game design. The "Metal Slug Hell Zone X" game also has some complex technical components underlying his design. Jorge discovered how to create a side-scrolling game and complicated types of animation by using a combination of difficult programming concepts, including variables, loops, conditional statements, communication and synchronization commands (such as broadcast and when-receive), and Boolean logic. These demonstrate a range of computer programming concepts (and a wide range of technology fluency) in the adoption of these concepts for use in his game.

FIGURE 4.3. Jorge's video game "Metal Slug Hell Zone X"

Finally, Jorge's project also moves beyond some of the connections to artistic and technical domains, to make connections to media education. For example, Jorge's video-game production provides insight into how the goals of media education apply to gaming. In this project, Jorge learned about game design through imitation, and as Buckingham (2003) points out, "imitation is an indispensable aspect of learning" in media education (p. 134). Beyond Jorge's attention to interface conventions, he explored, and in some senses reformulated, genre conventions of shooter games. The title denotes that his work is in the same series as other Metal Slug games (e.g., Metal Slug 2, Metal Slug X, and Metal Slug Advance), yet there seems to be a parodic edge to the title (Hell Zone X) because, while he has conformed to most of the trademarks of the series, Jorge's re-creation has an almost Zen-like impact on the viewer/player. Jorge's game lacks the loud music and sound effects of the original, and with animated clouds floating overhead and the rolling terrain beneath, the resounding quality of this game is one of tranquility and solitude. Jorge created no antagonists to shoot, no violence, no blood, and no chaos that we might otherwise expect in a "Hell Zone," and instead has focused on creating a smoothly animated protagonist and a space for this character to dwell. While some might question whether Jorge had the time or the know-how to do such things in Scratch, when we examine this case longitudinally, we actually discover that his earlier work contained all of these conventions, which were slowly subtracted from the game until it reached the point in the design process described in this chapter. This seems to be a play on the genre itself (simultaneously a violation and a creative act). Jorge told us that one of the reasons for coming to the Clubhouse included the sense of focus and calm that he experienced when he worked on his projects. In this sense, the game serves as a metaphor for

Jorge's everyday experiences and encapsulates the sense of relief that Jorge felt at the Clubhouse when he was engaged in his work.

LEARNING WITH SCRATCH ON MULTIPLE LEVELS

Through these case studies, we can see that youth are mixing a variety of media, genres, and ideas in Scratch. Learning to mix new media allows youth to build on their existing knowledge and learn about new epistemological domains of value to the larger society. This is particularly important as youth from under-served areas engage in after-school learning. At the Clubhouse, youth are able to build bridges between their cultural backgrounds as well as extend their understanding of domains that are outside of the typical offerings of low-income schools, such as computer science, art, and media education curricula. While these case studies describe the successful appropriation of Scratch within the South Los Angeles community, even a cursory look at the Scratch online archive gives one the sense that youth all over the globe are able to use this tool for personal expression, critical engagement, and the development of technical expertise.

This chapter demonstrates how media mixing within Scratch provides youth with a tool to develop several skill sets while simultaneously supporting prolonged engagement with projects that are often deeply individual and personally meaningful. Scratch is but one tool for media mixing, as youth doubtlessly mix media across a variety of software at the Clubhouse. Regardless of the platform, youth—especially ones the age of those in our case studies—are at a critical stage in the formation of their identities and often become disenchanted in both school and out-of-school settings with activities that do not allow them to build upon their preexisting interests. Being able to use one tool like Scratch for a variety of purposes (such as making art, animations, or video games) allows youth to make connections among different genres of work and different disciplinary domains, and allows youth to appropriate the software in a way that resonates both personally and culturally with them. For this reason, we add a third type of connection that youth make while engaging in Scratch—cultural connections—which are relations to a larger cultural context, whether it be youth culture in general or part of other specific cultures to which the youth belong (Peppler & Kafai, 2006).

Epistemological connections are varied and plentiful in the work created in Scratch. We have explored three broad areas here, including connections to the arts, media, and new technology made while engaging in work in Scratch. While there are countless other connections that youth make to math, science, and other areas beyond the arts, media, and computer science, these areas are particularly well suited for summarizing the media-rich aspects of Scratch. What is unique about the creative experiences in Scratch is that youth are able to create and animate their own images but they are also able to engage in a broader range of roles, from artist, to performer, to director, and more. While other types of production, such as video production, act in a similar manner, Scratch enables both individuals and collectives to engage in this type of work. We have also argued that, through production, youth are increasing their understanding of media more generally and becoming more critical and discriminating participants in the larger media landscape (Peppler & Kafai, 2007). As youth engage in Scratch, they comprehend which aspects of media are malleable and how interface design changes the user experience. In addition, these case studies illustrate how designers develop an understanding of how genres are products of social and cultural construction, and result from choices made during the creative process. At the core of the technical learning in Scratch is the building of computer programming conceptual understanding. These case studies illuminate how programming within a media and/or arts context is very different from a context of math and science. Programming in this context is less about code and more about personal and critical expression. In fact, as youth engage in Scratch they are learning to manipulate the medium of the computer to create their own software packages, which is the main advantage of using a suite of programming tools such as those found in Scratch.

While case studies of youth in the Computer Clubhouse give us only a partial understanding of the larger design culture, they do provide us with an understanding of how individuals are able to repurpose the design environment for personal expression. Media mixing with Scratch has implications for broadening the participation and applications of traditional programming courses in K–12, which tend to focus on mathematics and science. Additionally, media mixing with Scratch is an essential component to artistic expression in a digital era—a tool that has an arguably increasing importance for youth and society at large. These projects emphasize media applications that are all at the core of technology interests for youth and thus could provide new opportunities to encourage and broaden participation of youth from underrepresented groups to become designers and inventors with new technologies.

As youth become more comfortable with the media-mixing capabilities within Scratch, they begin to branch out and explore other areas such as the physical interfaces or sensors that they can incorporate into their work in Scratch. The MIT Media Lab has made Scratch Sensor Boards available through the Scratch Web site, which are reminiscent of LEGO Mindstorms kits, but the upcoming chapter (Chapter 5) presents some of the work that youth have been doing to create their own sensors and various types of input, moving away from the keyboard and mouse interfaces into a wider array of interfaces. In doing so, youth connect to a wider array of computer science, engineering, and science concepts, moving beyond what is just offered in the on-screen environment.

Interface Design with Hook-Ups

Amon Millner

Schools, homes, and Computer Clubhouses have become places in which children express themselves using crafts and computers. This chapter explores how Clubhouse members bring craft materials and computers together in new ways—by designing physical computer interfaces called *Hook-ups*. For example, a Clubhouse member constructed a physical flying saucer capable of controlling an interactive Scratch project displayed on a computer screen.

This chapter begin with a brief description of the flying saucer example to help explain how Hook-ups work. The motivation for the Hook-ups research project was to promote engagement and learning through digital actions with physical objects that can provide a natural foray into scientific concepts, design, and invention. Case studies highlight the Hook-up creations of three Clubhouse members and show how they each followed their own interests through the design of digital and physical realms. The chapter ends with a discussion of the ways in which Hook-ups unlock paths for learning across boundaries in Clubhouses and beyond.

HOW HOOK-UPS WORK

Nia, a 10-year-old Clubhouse member, designed and built a Hook-up that controlled an animated flying saucer in Scratch simply using two paper plates stapled together. Nia drew decorative lights around the outside of the plates and secured a pushbutton to the top plate (see Figure 5.1). She then extended her saucer into the digital realm by using Scratch to animate an abduction beam every time she pressed the pushbutton.

To make her interface, Nia used the core tool of any Hook-up project: the *Scratch Sensor Board*. This board is a printed circuit board that contains and connects a set of electronic components that detect changes to certain properties of its physical environment. The board reports digital information concerning changes in the physical environment to Scratch through a cable that connects the board to a computer's USB port.

The Scratch Sensor Board supports a variety of sensors—objects that react to environmental conditions by changing their own electrical properties. The boards

FIGURE 5.1. Nia's UFO Hook-up and Scratch program

use the computer to which they connect as a power source, supplying electric current to conductive paths throughout the board. Eight of those paths pass through
sensors. Four paths run through built-in sensors that change current flow according to light intensity, sound levels, a sliding shaft's position, and a pushbutton's
position, respectively. Another four paths run through (alligator) clip cables to
which sensors connect and disconnect. Clipped-on sensors range in application
from measuring temperature to detecting a board's degree of tilt. Young people
have utilized a variety of sensors to detect diverse aspects of their environments,
but the scope of this chapter includes interfaces using the type of sensor most
prevalent in Clubhouse member-made Hook-ups: switches.

Switches are mechanical devices, like Nia's pushbutton, that connect or break
parts of conductive paths in an electric circuit. The Scratch Sensor Boards measure
current along paths containing sensors. When a switch's mechanical state is such

that its contacts are apart, a Scratch Sensor Board notices an "open" circuit. When a board detects an open circuit, it changes the value of a block in Scratch labeled "sensor connected?" If a circuit is open, when a Scratch program encounters this block in a script, the block inquiring about the status of a sensor or switch receives "false" or "not connected." When a switch's contacts touch, a "closed" circuit results, and the "sensor-connected" block becomes "true" until the contacts separate.

Nia's script repeated continually as it moved a graphical saucer to a new screen location and checked if the pushbutton atop her physical saucer had been pressed. When the "if" block in her script received a "true" value from her sensor board via the "sensor-connected" block, a set of command blocks generated an abduction beam graphic. When "sensor-connected" was false, the script would bypass the blocks responsible for generating the abduction beam.

THE HOOK-UPS PROJECT MOTIVATION

The Hook-ups Project is motivated by questions concerning design, engagement, and learning: How can we design technological tools to enable a range of activities that combine physical and digital design processes? What kinds of connections to personal interests help novices become engaged in Hook-ups design? As youth engage in various styles of design, what concepts related to computing and physical design do they learn?

Building upon physical design experiences that dovetail with computational design provides new opportunities for youth to think and construct creatively. Having more creative opportunities prepares youth to thrive in a society in which the reach of computation is expanding in our working and learning environments, yet we still value rich learning through our physical senses. An increasing number of scientific fields, such as astronomy and earth and environmental sciences, are recognizing creative approaches to computing that influence their practices (Anthes, 2008). Youth will be at the helm of these budding fields involving computing. American inventor George Washington Carver argued that "new developments are the products of a creative mind, so we must therefore stimulate and encourage that type of mind in every way possible" (quoted in Kremer, 1991).

More recently, Richard Florida and Daniel Pink have led a growing number of authors urging that we extend the development of the creative mind into contemporary contexts (Florida, 2002), bringing attention to the "seismic—though as yet undetected—shift now underway in much of the advanced world" that will place "artists, inventors, designers and the like in a position to reap society's richest rewards and share its greatest joys" (Pink, 2006, p. 1). Hook-ups projects can foster young people's inventive and creative states of mind, building upon Papert's "objects-to-think-with" constructionist philosophy, as well as Pestalozzi's assertion that people learn best through the activation of their physical senses and physical activity (Pestalozzi, 1894).

The Hook-ups Project serves as an entry point for youth/novices to invent and design interactions between physical objects and computer programs. Eisenberg

(2003) argues that projects with such a focus should become a larger part of the learning research landscape. Integrated introductions to design allow youth to develop design skills, explore design strategies, and learn scientific concepts through multiple pathways.

PHYSICAL AND DIGITAL DESIGN OPPORTUNITIES AT CLUBHOUSES

The informal learning environment in Clubhouses is conducive for youth to explore ideas through designing and inventing using both physical and digital media. Members have combined physical and digital realms in projects using LEGO Mindstorms kits to enable physical objects to run computer programs that allow creations to dynamically interact with the physical world. The Hook-ups Project builds upon the research that led to Mindstorms, and differs by enabling youth to use physical objects to make interfaces to a computer's on-screen world. Another distinction is that the Mindstorms kit lends itself to LEGO brick-based projects using primarily LEGO-made sensors. Hook-ups are designed to connect with a wider variety of materials and sensors, providing members with multiple paths to learning.

CLUBHOUSE MEMBERS CREATING HOOK-UPS

In creating her flying saucer Hook-up, Nia made decisions that all Hook-ups creators face. Each interface creator chooses different sensors, materials, and programs from many possible options to build his or her desired interaction. Figure 5.2 illustrates the landscape of options for building a sample Hook-up: a radio interface. The Clubhouse youth (top right) choose to combine physical materials (top) with a combination of handmade or manufactured sensors (top left). The sample radio Hook-up (middle) reflects their choice to use a cardboard box as a form that features their artistic elements, a rotating knob sensor, and a toggle switch. Youth connect the radio's sensors to the Scratch Sensor Board (bottom) tethered to the laptop running Scratch (bottom right). They program Scratch to make a cat move when the switch position changes and a person rotates the knob.

The materials from which members select to form sensors and interface housings come from a supply of materials that already exist at a Clubhouse or supplies found elsewhere. On occasion, the materials and sensor types available inspire the Hook-up. In other cases, a project idea calls for a member to find specific materials.

The following three cases illustrate how Clubhouse members navigated the design space depicted in Figure 5.2. Each covers projects that used switches as sensors in unique interfaces and led to different outcomes. The first describes a Hook-up inspired by a drum. A slingshot influenced the second. The third features a clay-covered magnet capable of moving objects on a screen similarly to how a computer mouse works. The data collected for each of the cases consist of field notes that documented design activities and interactions between Charlestown

FIGURE 5.2. Hook-up's system elements

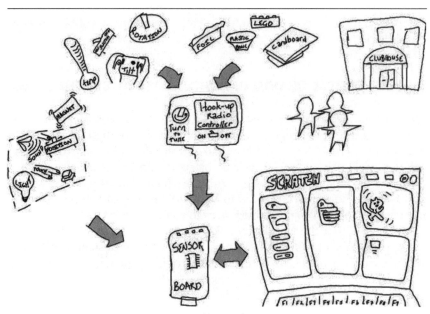

Computer Clubhouse members and mentors, saved Scratch programs, and Hook-up artifacts created by members. (A more detailed description of the Charlestown Computer Clubhouse can be found in Table I.1.)

Ray's Drum

In this Computer Clubhouse Ray was an ever-smiling 12-year-old rock-star-in-the-making who worked on a music project using unexpected materials to learn how switches could generate synthesized musical notes. Ray liked working with music at the Clubhouse and wanted to enhance an interactive band project he wrote in Scratch. He envisioned letting a user hit a physical drum mock-up to start animated drumming sequences and sounds. (His idea predated the popular drum- and guitar-driven Rock Band video game that influenced later Hook-ups.) Craft drawers at the Clubhouse supplied an assortment of traditional materials, such as Popsicle sticks, pipe cleaners, and packing peanuts, yet none of the materials looked suitable for making an instrument. While Ray did not discover what would become his drum in the craft drawer/area, he found a drumlike object, a CD spindle case, on the computer supply shelf. By turning office supplies into material for construction, Ray did what many designers do: He embraced the unexpected. Soon he discovered that the points at which the CD spindle case's base and top met could be transformed into a switch.

Ray experimented with adding foil to the CD case cover and base so that when people hit the cover, the two parts would meet, causing the metallic foil strips to meet. This contact would signal to the sensor board that the circuit was closed (and thus conducting current). In order for Scratch to detect that he was closing a circuit, Ray had to attach one sensor board clip head to the CD case's base-side foil strip and the other to the cover's foil strip, using wire to extend the cable's reach (see Figure 5.3). Ray watched the reading on the "sensor-connected" monitor in his Scratch project change between values of "true" (0% current resisted) when the cover was pressed and "false" (100% current resisted) when the cover was at rest above the base's foil. In order for Ray to make his switch's foil contact strips touch each other when a person struck his drum, he placed the strips in a location that would signal a circuit closing with a reasonable amount of reliability only when an actual strike occurred. Switch placement for reliability became an important design consideration.

Ray's strikes triggered Scratch scripts to make sounds that satisfied him. He then upgraded his Scratch band project to trigger digitally synthesized musical

FIGURE 5.3. Ray's spindle drum Hook-up and Scratch program

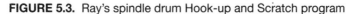
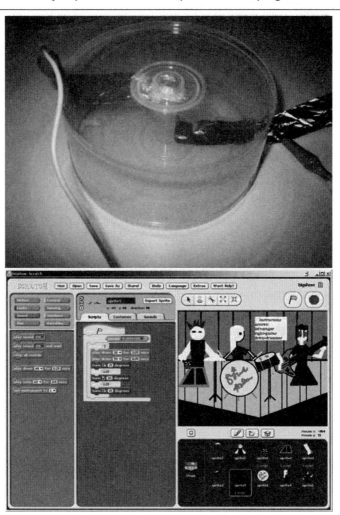

notes via physical drum strikes as opposed to the keyboard strokes that his project previously relied upon. His new script featured command blocks that only played sounds if the preceding conditional block detected "sensor-connected" to be true. His program played drum sounds and at the same time triggered an on-screen drummer to move his arms. Ray explored manipulating a switch to control current flowing through an open or closed circuit before ever learning about the concepts in a class. Ray worked with a mix of music, computation, and physical materials to make his first Hook-up.

Martin's Slingshot

Martin, a 13-year-old member who enjoyed stirring up activity in the Clubhouse, had fun flinging things. However, before he was introduced to Hook-ups, he couldn't do so without the risk of putting others in danger. He overcame several challenges as he built a complex slingshot Hook-up from simple parts and tweaked its tensile strength to have it control an interactive game.

Similarly to how Ray considered ways to integrate a handmade switch into an existing product's casing, Martin found after several tries an existing product that he could repurpose to serve as the base for his slingshot switch. Martin had to find his own parts. He looked around the Charlestown Clubhouse for ways to make a slingshot. Though he ran into difficulties, he ultimately gleaned an understanding of the design strategy of building complex things from simple parts.

Children looking to make a traditional slingshot are usually able to find a sturdy Y-shaped stick with two branches to stretch a rubber band across. The cold of Boston's winter made searching for an appropriate tree branch difficult for Martin. Instead, he searched around the Clubhouse. A clothespin he found seemed sturdy, yet he could not spread the wooden prongs far enough apart to make a convincing slingshot interface. Having access to multiple clothespins, he embarked on the mission to build a larger slingshot—one that would fit in his hand.

Martin clipped three clothespins together and added a bottle cap to spread them into a Y shape. He was surprised by how fast the multiclothespin structure fell apart when he pulled the rubber band he placed across its top. Onlookers were surprised to see clothespins flying and some offered their ideas for fixing the design (while a few others made fun of the mess). In Clubhouses these are the kinds of disruptions that create opportunities for mutual help and new ideas. A small group of members helped Martin reorient the clothespins several times. As is the case with many designs, iteration proved fruitful. The slingshot wasn't able to withstand a rubber band pull until the group removed the springs on each clothespin and reinserted them into a new location on the prongs. Martin placed springs in a way that secured two clothespins together. In a clothespin's normal use, the spring applies force to the wooden prong tips to provide enough tension to keep clothes on a clothesline. For a slingshot, clothespins didn't need tension to keep prongs closed; rather, they needed tension to keep three clothespins connected. Martin rearranged the springs, explored leverage points while repositioning springs, and ultimately added a switch to the slingshot rubber band so that he could (digitally) fling things at Scratch objects. Martin clamped a pair of sensor board clip heads to the front and rear sides of the rubber band (see Plate 15). When the rear side of the rubber band was pulled back and released, the exposed metallic parts of the clip heads came into contact and closed a circuit. Martin wrote a Scratch program that recognized when the switch was closed and propelled a digital object across the computer screen toward a digital duck—an adaptation of an interactive program written by his peers for a different Hook-up.

Kerry's Clay Mouse Emulator

Kerry, a reserved 13-year-old, turned an interest in clay and magnets into a way of understanding how some computer programs coordinate events. The Clubhouse setting gave him freedom to explore a project with no particular end in sight. As he adopted a bricoleur approach (Turkle & Papert, 1990) to designing his clay mouse emulator, Kerry was free to dynamically change project directions. His project benefited from clay, magnets, and computers—each being in close proximity to one another.

Kerry realized that magnets and reed switches were parts of the material that Hook-up researchers/mentors brought to Charlestown (among other materials and sensors to augment a Clubhouse's collection of crafts and sensors). We explained how these switches worked in a context with which Kerry was familiar. A reed switch is commonly found on door and window frames lying adjacent to a magnet affixed to the closed door or window. When a typical building alarm is armed, the system senses when a door or window is opened by noticing that the magnet is no longer keeping the frame's reed switch closed (i.e., the two objects have separated).

Before doing any project planning, Kerry experimented with distances at which magnet pairs would attract and repel. The distance gave him an idea of how far apart he had to place reed switches so that two did not simultaneously close due to one magnet. He used his measurement to arrange four reed switches under a plate so that no single magnet could close more than one switch. Kerry connected the switches to clip heads on a Scratch Sensor Board. He modified a Scratch program he saw a peer using to make a character on the screen move in different directions when one of the hidden reed switches closed due to a nearby magnet.

Kerry realized that his Hook-up worked similarly to a computer mouse—it could fluidly move objects on the screen. He became enamored with designing something quickly that worked somewhat like an item he could buy (a mouse) yet wanted to give it personality. He found it difficult to mimic the curvy shape of the mouse on the computer nearest to him using paper. A plastic bowl was too bulky. He discovered that he could mold a lump of sculpting clay into the mouse shape he desired. He wedged a magnet into the bottom of his mold and added decorative eyes to the top to serve as fake mouse buttons. What he created was not only a piece of art, but a means for him to explore magnetism and computation (see Figure 5.4).

Just as a magnet can influence multiple objects around it, a Scratch block can broadcast information to influence other objects. Each object can choose to react to the information or ignore it. Kerry attempted to use his understanding of magnetism to understand broadcasting. He envisioned Scratch objects communicating with each other similarly to how he imagined magnets communicate. He could

FIGURE 5.4. Kerry's magnet-carrying mouse Hook-up and Scratch program

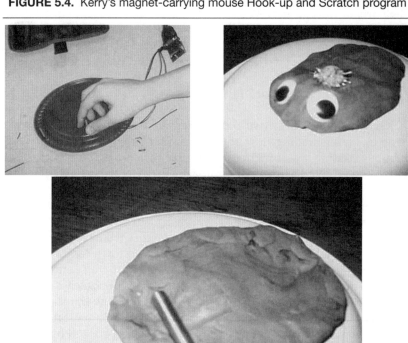

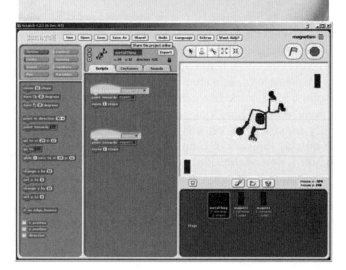

imagine magnets broadcasting messages to other magnets. One end of a magnet could broadcast a message, "come to me," while the end of a nearby magnet is always listening for that message. When the second magnet's end hears the message, it responds with an action, moving toward the broadcaster. Kerry drew a character that was holding what appeared to be metal silverware. He programmed the character to respond to "magnet-on" and "magnet-off" broadcasts. Kerry had the freedom to explore how magnetic fields could influence physical and digital objects and to experience how digital objects passed information to each other.

HOOK-UPS POSSIBILITIES IN CLUBHOUSES AND BEYOND

In combining craft materials and computers to make interfaces, Nia, Ray, Martin, and Kerry followed their interests through diverse project trajectories. The rest of this chapter considers how they became exposed to concepts in design, physics, engineering, and computer science, and shows how such interdisciplinary projects transform spaces (in Clubhouses and beyond) into resources for creating projects and developing creative minds.

Ray's interest in music shaped his Hook-ups experience. He had already created several Scratch projects, so he eagerly seized the opportunity to extend a music-based project into the physical world. In brainstorming plans for his drum Hook-up, he initially sought to make a multiple-drum set. Helping members like Ray, who wish to start a project that mirrors or simulates a nontrivial activity, is challenging. Activities such as Ray's drumming have multiple components that make the actual experience of playing them rich. It is difficult to determine which components of activities are conducive to designing a tractable initial Hook-up.

Balancing tractability and challenge, while at the same time promoting authentic interaction, is an elusive yet valuable goal for those facilitating Clubhouse activities. Facilitating an appropriate first step opens the door for further steps. As soon as Martin finished his slingshot he began working with a group on a related Hook-up. Should a member continue to work on a project beyond a simplified initial interface, he or she will be calling upon understandings of the Hook-ups toolkit gleaned while building the initial interface. Exploring how switches work and/or creating a custom switch served as an appropriate starting step in the Hook-ups cases discussed here.

Ray did not consider it a complex activity to place foil at strategic locations within a discarded CD case to create a switch. An experienced designer would consider Ray's switch to be simple. By contrast, parts of Martin's project called for him to exercise the design strategy of building complex behaviors from simple parts. Martin's slingshotlike Hook-up only came together when he built a structure larger and stronger than a single clothespin by combining three of them.

Building Martin's Hook-up exposed him to concepts relating to multiple fields. Like the project paths of the other Hook-up creators discussed, Martin's involved controlling electric current through a switch. Additionally, he worked with his hands to explore the tension and tensile strength of his construction materials—squeezing and tweaking them to find potential breaking points. These topics from mechanical engineering and physics, coupled with the computer programming topics he encountered, allowed him to explore all-too-often disparate disciplines.

Ray's path to creating his Hook-up included musical, electrical, and computational components. Kerry's combined sculpting, magnetism, and computation. Kerry explored magnetic fields with sensors and digital animations. His project was more distinctive than the common classroom activity of using magnets to move iron shavings around. The latter helps people visualize the effects of a magnetic field. In Kerry's case, Scratch offered a dynamic way to visualize how magnets influence objects.

Our Hook-ups creators' diverse paths arrived at computing through physical design paths based on different interests. The computing concepts they explored also differed. While sensor-based projects typically call for their creators to work with conditional statements (such as, if "sensor-connected," do this—a fundamental computing concept), the members confronted other computer science topics as well.

Martin learned about conditional statements by reusing Scratch scripts that he saw his friends create. In adapting the script he inherited, he had to familiarize himself with the concept of *code reuse.* He examined the workings of his peers' interactive game to adapt it to his needs. A common practice among programmers is to build complex computer applications by working with less complex chunks of code, often coming from other people. The vast libraries of code available for established programming languages, such as Python, are a testament to the popularity of the code reuse concept.

Martin's efforts to create a new interface for a project built on his peer's prior work demonstrate the utility of a project-sharing community. Clubhouses often keep members' files in a shared space where everyone can access art, music, and programs. In a classroom setting, borrowing a peer's work to start a project is less prevalent.

Starting from a blank Scratch screen (rather than a friend's sample), Kerry explored passing information between objects in his Scratch program in a way that made sense to him: a conversation between magnets. Two magnets talking would not likely be an illustrative example for the part of a computer science course syllabus concerning interobject communication.

It seems unlikely that Nia's, Ray's, Martin's, and Kerry's schools could support projects that involved students combining computers and physical materials. K–12 schools and colleges alike are asked to arrange their resources to educate large groups of diverse students. Traditional teachers in these formal settings are charged with ensuring that their students become acquainted with core concepts of a course. In contrast, a Clubhouse coordinator focuses on helping members to explore their particular interests in projects of their own choosing.

Clubhouse coordinators should play a distinct role in supporting members' interests and approaches, and yet at times coordinators have facilitated activities in ways that were not conducive to Hook-ups work. For example, coordinators who question their ability to understand the intersection of computing and craft have sometimes shied away from providing support to members who take on such activities—even in nontechnical regards, such as encouragement or access to materials. In certain cases coordinators have remedied lackluster support for projects fusing computers and crafts by increasing their comfort with new Clubhouse activities or sharing facilitating duties with assistants, available mentors, and advanced members. When these groups provide flexible support, members have more guides for interdisciplinary explorations like the cases represented in this chapter.

Current United States policies for funding schools in low-income communities make it difficult for teachers to purchase and manage materials, given subpar facilities and pressure to meet controversial academic benchmarks (Kozol, 1991; Sampson, 2007). The projects illustrated in this chapter demonstrate how youth can find suitable craft and recycled materials in unusual places, thus reducing the material procurement hurdle for schools interested in adopting Hook-ups activities. With any materials that art studios, physics labs, or cafeterias provide, more Hook-ups activities become possible either during or after school. Inviting youth to integrate recycled objects, digital media, and items from their homes into projects encourages them to view the space around computers in new ways. They begin to merge sensors with (or make sensors from) everyday materials that they would not normally associate with computers. Creating associations between computers and physical objects with which children have existing relationships changes their relationship to computing. Projects like Hook-ups that link computing with items that a child considers familiar are a step toward making the world of computing more widely familiar.

In a study that Margolis and Fisher (2003) conducted to examine why women (and underrepresented groups in general) represent only a small percentage of college students studying computer science, they note factors such as lack of experience. Because males and females of both struggling and affluent backgrounds generally gain experience constructing objects from crafts and found materials at early ages, using such materials to make interfaces for computers ensures that a range of children have a familiar starting point in the activity. A factor that helps mitigate the experience gap in Hook-ups activities is the novelty of controlling digital worlds with as many physical objects as one can find. Creating objects that control computers is an activity to which children are unlikely to have been exposed.

Establishing personal connections between youth who are underrepresented in traditional computer science and new fields stemming from computing is critical. Researchers and organizations like Computer Clubhouses must play an important role in preparing youth to advance the growing number of fields that computing influences. Doing so would heed Carver's call to action about developing creative minds early.

This chapter explored how children at Computer Clubhouses are designing and building their own physical computer interfaces called Hook-ups and discussed several initial outcomes of the Hook-ups research project in Computer Clubhouse settings. Three case studies (and an extended example) illustrated how members created physical interfaces to digital projects and, by doing so, connected themselves to computing, scientific concepts, design, and inventing. The kinds of explorations at the intersection of computing, broad interest, and everyday materials that the Hook-ups project helped introduce to Clubhouses are steps toward preparing today's youth to fully participate in the creative society that authors Florida and Pink have projected for the future.

NOTES

Information about building or ordering sensor boards that communicate with Scratch is available at the Scratch Web site (http://scratch.mit.edu). Click on the "forums" or "support" links and then click on the phrase "sensor boards."

Chapter 6

Youth Video Productions of Dance Performances

Kylie Peppler and Yasmin Kafai

In this chapter we turn to video productions and dance performances that are popular among youth in the Computer Clubhouses. Often in organizing videos and performing these dances, Clubhouse members demonstrate the type of youth leadership and initiative that is common across the Clubhouse Network. While dance happened to be a popular mode of expression in the South Los Angeles Clubhouse, many of the other Clubhouses report that youth engage in collaborative beat mixing or music making, which pulls in large groups of young people in a similar manner.

Across the Network, some of the most extensive interests include dance and music making. Instead of neglecting the cultural innovations taking place around the Clubhouse, the space is infused by them, allowing members to build upon their interests to document local community practices from the ground up. This is often very different from introducing a set of new tools or practices—like the ones described with Scratch in previous chapters—that originated in another culture.

To illustrate how Clubhouse youth engage collaboratively we delve into the culture of dance productions and performances in the Youth Opportunities Unlimited (Y.O.U.) Inc. Computer Clubhouse in South Los Angeles. In particular, we draw upon the Krump dance movement and the local performances at the Clubhouse, where members organized, videotaped, and edited collaborative dance circles, often involving 30 to 40 Clubhouse members. Krump, often associated with Clowning, is a dance style brought to mainstream attention by the documentary, *Rize* (LaChappelle, 2005). Krump originated in South Los Angeles and references African dance forms in what is commonly seen as positive expressions of anger or releases of pent-up emotion. The dance itself can be characterized by free, expressive, and highly energetic moves. As Krump is a popular feature of many music videos, members at this Clubhouse experiment with their own documentation techniques, not relying on outsiders to capture and edit their story. The efforts of urban youth to find an artistic outlet for expression can help us understand how youth organize and engage in learning activities. In addition, paying attention to local funds of knowledge can turn our attention to successful practices in low-income communities that so often are portrayed as deficient in resources and agency.

CLUBHOUSE KRUMPING

The Krump culture evolved in the Clubhouse space as youth merged their dance practices and their technology interests—each informing the other. Youth created and filmed hundreds of dance videos at the Clubhouse, moving from dance to other aspects of production, including recording, editing, and staging these events. Over the 4 years of our observations at the Youth Opportunities Unlimited Inc. Computer Clubhouse, we counted more than 250 homemade videos stored on their server. Numerous field notes written by mentors documented dance performances and recordings as part of daily Clubhouse activities. We use a series of smaller vignettes to describe how Krumping was part of the youth organizing efforts of the Computer Clubhouse members, an example of where the youth were able to successfully organize themselves during the course of our observations. The various facets of the youths' capture of the dance activities are explored and presented with excerpts from the field notes and screen captures of the youth engaged in the making of the dance videos. We explored three aspects of the Clubhouse Krump culture that we felt were important to better understanding youth organizing, collaboration, and community development: critique and expertise, the division of labor, and the cultural perspectives of insiders/outsiders on these events.

The following is an edited version of several field notes that were written by four different mentors, describing the same day's events (May 2, 2006) at the Computer Clubhouse. In this vignette, the mentor comes into the room and notices a group of young people around the computer. The mentor then discovers that the youth are working on editing a dance video from one of their previous dance performances. Kaylee takes on the role of the editor, in part because she is the only one at the site with the technological know-how to do this.

> *Viewing and Editing the Artifact.* When I first came into the Clubhouse
> I noticed around seven of the younger members crowded over one of
> the computers. They were all watching a dance video that they created
> last Thursday. I walked around and noticed that Kaylee wanted to look
> through the dance video and edit certain clips out. In the video, I saw a
> circle of members with one member dancing in the middle. The youth
> took turns coming into the middle of the circle to dance in front of the
> camera. The dances ranged from Krumping to breaking, to other styles.
> The kids seemed really interested in the movie because they were debating what clips to keep and how to improve it.

One of the key organizational attributes of the dance is the idea of the circle. The circle has been prominent in dance cultures around the world but nevertheless is an important way for the youth to organize. By forming a circle while dancing, it places everyone on an equal plane until someone chooses to take the center of the circle, at which point they take the lead. This places an importance on individual agency within the group and at the same time places everyone on equal footing. The editing of the video, additionally, becomes an important site for learning. The youth critique the performance, the camera angles, and the best way to edit the video. The contribution of the technology to this activity is twofold: (1) as an artifact for documentation and as a tool for reflection beyond the ephemeral dance performance; and (2) as an additional mode of expression beyond the dance itself, allowing for more youth to participate in the viewing and editing process, even if they were not in the original dance production.

> *The Dance Performance.* After painting their faces, the youth were ready to record again. When the DJ played the song "Gimme That" by Chris Brown . . . two members, one African American right around age 7 or 8 and another member . . . initiated the video and the rest were soon to follow. Each member went in front of the camera and started dancing. They all performed individually with different styles of break dancing, while the girls focused on incorporating the hip-hop-like dance moves that were completely different from the moves of the boys. When they started recording, the younger members were very intrigued at being able to see themselves on screen and for others to see them as well. The younger ones would constantly take turns going in front of the camera, making funny faces or posing at different angles. I asked the older girls, "So what role do you serve in this project?" and Ebony answered, "Well, we have to make sure that the younger ones know what they are doing. We can't have them screwing up our dances by them just doing whatever. We have to keep them in line." It was clear that these two knew their roles in the project, yet the group was still flexible enough to accept new members. I saw a brand-new member getting in line with the other dancers.

These descriptions point to some important aspects of this work. Just as in the well-known samba schools in South America that Papert (1993b) used as an example for successful learning cultures, there are multiple opportunities for apprenticeship. In this example, the older members show the younger ones how to participate and structure the activity through their efforts to choreograph the dances and keep the younger members in line. However, in one of the later field-note excerpts the reader will see that this type of top-down mentorship isn't always the case. Breona, one of the youngest members, is actually the star dancer and the other members learn from and are inspired by her dance moves.

CRITIQUE AND EXPERTISE

The judgments of the quality of dance invite critique—for better or worse—of how successful a particular dance move is or how expert the member is in Krump technique. Video enables youth to immediately review their performances. This next excerpt demonstrates that the younger members have a valuable contribution to the innovation in the activity.

> *Critique, Expertise, and Self-Confidence.* While the younger members were performing, the older ones watched and critiqued, giving opinions or

laughing at the boys who "danced funny" or "looked retarded." After the song was over they decided to ask one African American girl, named Breona, to participate in the video. She mentioned that she needed to hear a different song and suggested a song by Missy Elliot called "Lose Control." She was so good; it was no wonder why the guys were so intimidated by her. The other members also acknowledged the younger members who were good dancers. Breona was complimented on her dance moves. She received comments like "dang that girl can dance," from the older members. Her dance moves were more crisp and fluid than the other two girls'. I was greatly impressed at how talented Breona was. She was way more proficient at dancing and had more confidence than any of the other girls. One of the other girls, Ebony, who was in charge of the choreography for the girls, was very outspoken and seemed like she could dance really well, but when it came down to performing for the music video, she became very self-conscious and seemed to dance poorly on purpose. Ebony was older than Breona, yet because of Breona's carefree viewpoint she was able to perform with ease.

This excerpt points to the multiple opportunities for innovation—a highly valued contribution in Krump culture. The activity itself is open enough to allow for infinite degrees of innovation both in the filming and in the choice of dance moves—a high ceiling—and yet allows for new members without much experience to be involved as well—a low floor. The structure of several consecutive dances, each only a few minutes in length, allows for members to enter and leave the activity as needed. This feature also allows for multiple entry points, in case it takes the kids a while to warm up to the activity. In addition, the Krump culture, similar to what was found in samba schools, allows for and encourages cross-gender and cross-age participation. The youth are united by their shared goals: the performance and the documentation. Finally, the activity itself is easily expandable from a group of 6–7 youth to a group of 30 youth at times and leads to multiple ways to contribute to the activity.

DIVISION OF LABOR

The Clubhouse dance video activity presents multiple opportunities for youth to draw upon their individual areas of expertise and take on strong leadership roles. In the following field-note excerpt, the division of labor is explored. Several of the youth take on leadership roles, including Dwight and Javan, as the producer and director, respectively. In addition, there are several other roles that youth step up to fill, including the role of DJ (FAFA), makeup artist (Javan), choreographer (Ebony), editor (Kaylee), and dancers (e.g., Breona and several college mentors). Each of these roles is interdependent on the other.

Roles. The dance group included only three girls, all of whom were African American. The rest of the group contained six boys, both African

American and Latino. One of the older members, Javan, took on the role of the director. I talked to Javan earlier, and he said that he did all the planning and face painting. All of the boys in the group had their faces painted with different designs by Javan. Though Javan organized the sequence of events for the music video, each member involved had his or her own role. There was a designated role for each *member:* One was the DJ in charge of the music, another was in charge of recording the video, another was the producer, another the choreographer, another was the editor, and the remainder were dancers.

Although the collaborative activity can take place in the absence of any one member because the leadership is distributed, each member plays an important role in shaping the project. Roles are divided up according to interest and ability. For example, Kaylee's knowledge of the video-editing software facilitated her involvement in the group as the editor.

INSIDERS VS. OUTSIDERS:
VIEWS ON AGGRESSION IN THE DANCE CULTURE

Learning to Krump and participating in the dance events requires some basic cultural knowledge and an understanding of the shared importance of the event. Despite being a fairly open group—and this is where a sense of agency comes in when an individual chooses to participate in the dance activity or not—the activity is not necessarily understandable to cultural outsiders. In fact, the aggressive qualities of the dance and the acted battling that sometimes takes place during dance-offs or visual displays of anger can be frightening to outsiders who don't understand the cultural meaning behind these activities. The members themselves share an understanding of the importance of the activity and accept these displays of violence as a form of expression and not of aggression.

In sum, Krumping knowledge is situated and context-specific: Insiders in the activity see the visual displays as countering feelings of oppression while outsiders see it as a form of aggression. While the context varies, this seems to be the case with most collaborative activities. Members join together because of a shared interest while outsiders to the activity see it as deviant or unhealthy. This tension between insiders and outsiders in collaborative activities is highlighted in the following two field-note excerpts, both written by Latino males who were undergraduate mentors at the field site during this same time.

> *Insider.* I was especially surprised when I saw her dancing as if she was calling out one of the members to battle her . . . . Breona got right in Dwight's face and pretended to be slashing him and ripping him apart through her battling. This whole idea of women being nice and sweet and not really showing hostility but tranquility was completely false. This young girl was ready to challenge any male who challenged her way of dancing because she knew that she was confident enough to chal-

lenge the boys to dance. At one point I decided to come into the film and relive my youth. I did a few break-dancing moves. The kids seemed to have enjoyed watching me dance because they were cheering me on.

Outsider. One of them asked me if I could dance; I just nodded my head [to signify "no"]. I tried to get FAFA's [a male member's] attention but I called him FAT FAT. (O.C. I guess that I misheard his name because Kaylee and her friend laughed at that and repeated what I had said. FAFA seemed embarrassed. He smiled but he wasn't laughing and he seemed quieter than usual). I then noticed that the kids were dancing. They formed a circle, like in the video. I then saw two members, Daniel and FAFA play fighting. I wasn't sure what to do at that point, but I noticed that the Clubhouse coordinator looked over, laughed, and remarked, "Those boys are crazy." Her reaction made me feel that it was OK that they were doing this. I love the fact that they are bringing music into the Clubhouse in this manner, but it makes me feel uncomfortable that they were play fighting. I guess I didn't say anything because it seemed okay with the Clubhouse coordinator.

The mentor who is characterized as the insider uses terminology specific to the event (e.g., *battling*), participates by dancing (albeit break dancing and not Krumping), and reads Breona's aggressive gestures as empowering her as a female. By contrast, the mentor who is characterized as an outsider in this activity system is unsure of how to read the social context, relies on cues from an authority figure to know what is and is not appropriate, does not participate in the dance, and mistakenly calls the youth by an insulting version of his rapper name. Surprisingly, this mentor has been involved for over a year at the Clubhouse while the insider mentor is new to the Clubhouse activities.

Ironically, this activity, in contrast with most of the work at the Computer Clubhouse that can sometimes end in frequent feuds and hurt feelings, did not inspire any verbal (or otherwise) fighting among the members. In fact, the dance videos rallied the members and created a sense of community in the space. During the peak of the dance video movement, attendance was at an all-time high, the place was filled with music, and all of the youth were engaged in some aspect of creative production related to Krumping.

While the girls and boys maintained separate dance styles, they were working together toward the same creative ends. The girls in particular were able to regain a sense of control and presence in the Clubhouse activities through dance. In contrast to the misogyny often found in hip-hop cultures, the Krump circles allowed the girls to express physical violence in play form, giving them an acceptable outlet for their anger and aggression, which is often reserved only for males.

THE FLUIDITY OF ROLES

Our observations and analyses of Krumping indicate several distinct features from traditional small-group collaboration, which is the more common form of group work found in schools (Cohen, 1994). For example, we observed that members assumed multiple roles, and did so fluidly as they shifted from participants to observers to directors to editors and back. At least on the outset, there seemed to be less of a hierarchy based on authority of age, even though some club members pointed out that they needed to make sure that the younger ones knew what they were doing. Instead, fuller forms of participation seemed to derive from the dance performance itself, and so younger members could assume authority they would otherwise be denied in more traditionally organized settings. Most small-group collaborations have roles assigned even if participants cycle through them; here members adopt whichever role is needed and available, such as when they move in and out a circle during their Krumping performances.

In the previous chapters in Part II of this book, we examined the individual explorations of Clubhouse youth. While this is an important aspect of creative constructions, it neglects to describe the larger collaborative work that is taking place in these spaces. While we explored how certain ideas can act like *memes* (Dawkins, 1976), defined as ideas that take on a viral quality, spreading across the Network such as in the Cosmo puppet example found in Chapter 2, here we take a closer look at how collaborative activity can take place within an individual Clubhouse, forming what sociologists call *neo-tribes* (Bennett, 1999). Rather than fixed social groups, neo-tribes are fluid associations of collaborative groups and in this case help to describe the temporal groups that form at the Clubhouse, united, at least temporarily, in a common interest in music or dance. Youths' collaborative work is often influenced by the local context and frequently showcases finely tuned youth leadership skills, as these projects are mostly conceived of and executed by Clubhouse youth, leaving adults on the sidelines. These projects are also often highly innovative, drawing on the latest developments in music, dance, and other forms of media mixing.

What we saw in these dance performances and video productions at the Y.O.U. Inc. Clubhouse connects well to a growing body of work on youth activism, which has demonstrated the extent of political influence that disenfranchised youth can have on effecting social change (Cervone, 2002; Sherman, 2002). More recently this work has focused on youth activism as a context for learning and development (Kirshner, 2007) and has described four distinctive qualities of learning environments in youth activism groups, which map closely onto the Clubhouse environment. These qualities include (1) collective problem solving, (2) youth—adult interaction, (3) exploration of alternative frames for identity, and (4) bridges to academic and civic institutions—all of which overlap with core features of the Clubhouse model. In the case of the collaborative Krump culture, we can see here that youth are able to exercise leadership skills while engaging in twenty-first century-learning skills, such as those in learning to use video documentation for learning. As they do so, they are learning to write and document the stories in ways that can communicate the standpoints and values of their local community to others in distant communities.

PART III

COLLABORATIONS
IN THE CLUBHOUSE COMMUNITY

IN THIS PART we consider how various modes of collaboration within the Clubhouse community impact learning and creativity, whether within a single Clubhouse or across the entire Clubhouse Network. The first chapter of this section, written by Robbin Chapman, examines how incorporating critical reflection into Clubhouse learning activities can result in richer learning experiences for both members and mentors. She developed the Pearls of Wisdom software that engages members in critical reflection on their Clubhouse projects and learning experiences by creating and sharing artifacts called *Pearls.* The chapter outlines how members gained fluency with critical reflection and developed insights into their learning processes, and how their artifacts proliferated throughout the Clubhouse community. Chapman presents findings about patterns of reflective practices and discusses the implications of this emergent community practice for the learning and relationships that develop at the Clubhouse.

In the next chapter, Yasmin Kafai, Shiv Desai, Kylie Peppler, Grace Chiu, and Jesse Moya examine the nature of mentoring at the Clubhouse and how it informs our view of mentor roles and engagement. They present the notion of mentoring partnerships, defining these partnerships in terms of the varying interaction dynamics observed between mentors and members at the Clubhouse. Kafai posits that Clubhouse mentoring requires openness to new ways of interacting with youth, to learning new technologies, and to forming learning relationships. This rich mentoring palette runs the gamut from facilitator to observer to teacher to learner. Mentors who gained fluency with these varying roles were able to engage in the coconstruction and facilitation activities that best supported learning at the Clubhouse. Implications of the study underscore an important feature of the Clubhouse mentor model. While it is often assumed that mentors must be technically proficient to be effective, examination of Clubhouse mentoring implies youth and mentors can learn alongside one another.

The section's final chapter, written by Elisabeth Sylvan, delves into an aspect of Clubhouse community often difficult to measure: how members influence each others' learning and creativity through their connections to one another. Sylvan examined the nature of the flow of communication on the Clubhouse Village, the private intranet where over 5,000 active members share and showcase their design projects and ideas. She developed the Village Profile Survey software that captured and mapped who is participating, the nature of that participation, and how communication clustered around particular topics of relevance to the Clubhouse community. The chapter concludes with a discussion of the implications of her analyses of member connections, including how Clubhouse members from across the globe are discovering commonalities, both learning and social, with each other.

The findings shared in this section offer insights into how community-level collaborations can strengthen established methods of and provide new pathways to learning and teaching. The Clubhouse model is intended to promote constructive participation and sharing, both of member projects and of ideas. The work shared in these three chapters suggests that this remains true whether those collaborations occur face-to-face or online. Interestingly, peer sharing at the Clubhouse exists as a provocative combination of technology- and human-driven interaction. Whether project or socially focused, the Clubhouse learning experience is strengthened by both perspectives.

Chapter 7

Encouraging Peer Sharing: Learning Reflections in a Community of Designers

Robbin Chapman

At the core of constructionist learning at the Clubhouse is the idea that people learn through design experiences and sharing those designs and experiences with others. This would mean Clubhouse members would go beyond the activities of construction and reflect on their learning. However, deep reflection is more than just descriptive. It requires learners to slow down, critically examine their learning experiences, identify significant learning moments, and make sense of the learning that occurred. Having a tangible instantiation of their reflective process can enable learners to have subsequent opportunities to revisit their initial reflective episode. This deep reflection leads to transformative learning experiences where learners gain awareness of their own personal learning processes and transform those processes as they develop (Brown, 1994; Perkins, 1986; Schön, 1983). But it is rare for Clubhouse members to revisit their work to reflect on their design or learning processes, nor is reflection integrated as a regular practice.

I created a social knowledge sharing software called Pearls of Wisdom that helped members create, edit, and share design experiences in the form of reflective artifacts called *Pearls* (Chapman, 2006). A Pearl enables learners' thinking to be visible, tangible objects. Its purpose is to make possible the revisiting of learners' reflections on their learning and design processes. Design activities promote various forms of learning by engaging learners in a cycle of design, evaluation, and redesign. These activities tend to be authentic and ill-structured, requiring learners to interact with a variety of materials, tools, and ideas. During that process learners gain an understanding of those concepts related to achieving their design objectives (Perkins, 1986). Pearls represent both the process and product of learner reflection; they are a concrete instantiation of how and why learners know and what they consider meaningful about their learning.

Pearl design transforms transient occurrences of reflection into tangible artifacts that can be revised and shared. During Pearl construction, members must identify and revisit key learning experiences and organize those into some meaningful, coherent structure. That process requires consideration of content development, communication styles, and critical thinking to tell their learning story. As

Bruner (1996) has argued, articulating learning stories provides a way for learners to organize their experiences and make sense of their learning. The Pearl becomes an "object-to-reflect-with" in Papert's terms (1980); it facilitates the conversion of previous learning experiences into new, more complex learning insights. The following sections provide examples of different learning reflections, describe patterns of participation in the Flagship Clubhouse community during a one-year ethnographic study, and examine how individual and collaborative Pearl constructions became part of Clubhouse practices.

The study took place at the Flagship Computer Clubhouse in Boston, Massachusetts. A total of 305 young people from under-served communities participated and ranged in age from 10–12-year-olds (18%), 13–15-year-olds (35%), 16–18-year-olds (46%), and nonrespondents (1%). Mentors hailed from diverse backgrounds, both culturally and professionally, and possessed differing levels of mentoring experience.

THE NATURE OF PEARLS

The Pearl interface was designed to prompt the learners' reflective thinking by focusing attention on various epistemological aspects of their Clubhouse project including sources of their creativity, insights into the nature of their knowing and knowledge development, and understanding of the productive aspects of their design process. The Pearl user interface is divided into three panels, each with a header in the form of a first-person statement. The "Here's My Project" panel prompts members to either describe what their project is or include a project sample. The "What I'm Thinking About" panel prompts designers to share nonoperational aspects of their projects, such as their motivations for working on the project, insights from debugging episodes, or significant "ah-ha" learning moments. The "How I Did It" panel prompts the learner to discuss how the project was assembled (see Plate 16).

In Plate 16, the member customized the headers, number of pages, and the panel colors and sizes of her Pearl. An additional feature, the Pearl link, allows references to existing Pearls to be embedded. Linking facilitates existing Pearls to be referenced to create a more complex, composite Pearl. For example, existing Pearls on specific Photoshop graphics software features can be embedded into a new Pearl about a more complex Photoshop project that uses those features.

LEARNING REFLECTIONS IN PEARLS

How Clubhouse members articulated reflection in the "How I Did It" panels can be characterized by three modes of communication—algorithmic, heuristic, or anecdotal—or some combination of them. Algorithmic pearls provided detailed, ordered instructions on how use software to replicate the project. Heuristic Pearls provided less detail and used general "rule of thumb" insights. Anecdotal Pearl content was primarily self-promotion, broadcasting opinions, or idea storage.

Most members used the "What I'm Thinking About" panel to share learning insights, project motivations, or other information. One member shared her inspiration for making comics:

> I like making comic strips when I'm bored, or whenever I find a thought in my head that I think is funny. I can make them whenever I can use a computer.

Another member shared:

> Everytime I got into Google images to get cool ideas for new projects on Photoshop I am surprised of how fairy goddesses look. They are so beautiful, peaceful, mysterious, and perfect. So I decided to make myself look a little like them. Just a little! Remember that it is just Photoshop doing the magic, nobody in this world is perfect.

General themes were also shared, for example, "This title, Afro-kin, signifies the origin of people of all races and how at one point we were at peace with one another," or "My favorite season is spring. It smells so good outside and everything seems bright and fresh. I'm going to make some greeting cards with this project for my nana and mom."

The Pearl represents a persistent, editable recording of learner reflection. This enabled designers to take their time in refining or adding content. At any given time, the Pearl collection presented a snapshot of what design and project ideas the community was currently thinking about. Over time the collection charted the rise or demise of the ideas, popular design activities, and projects that resonated within the community.

PATTERNS OF PEARL PRACTICES

This study investigated how Pearl practices promoted a culture of Clubhouse members reflecting on their design and learning activities (Chapman, 2006). Like all Clubhouse activities, making Pearls was voluntary. During the study, 78 Pearls were created and 2,764 Pearl pages were viewed. Clubhouse members were asked to rate Pearl usefulness along two dimensions: breadth and depth. High breadth was considered a favorable rating because it marked a departure from the kind of Clubhouse project sharing seen in face-to-face member interactions, where members primarily helped one another with specific software features. While members helped others with parts of projects, assisting in the completion of an entire project was extremely rare. Of the Pearls reviewed, 81% were rated high for breadth indicating members opted to share a broader array of detail about their projects with the rest of the Clubhouse members, while 14% were rated medium, and 5% were rated low. Thus members were motivated to provide the necessary content so other members could reproduce entire projects, not just a particular software feature or subset of the project.

High-depth Pearls contained comprehensive explanations of software use to produce the project. Medium-depth Pearls contained important steps for making the project, with no information on software use. Of the Pearls reviewed, 64% rated medium depth indicating members opted to give just enough information to bootstrap project replication, while 14% of Pearls were high depth and 22% were low depth.

Pearl scoring and survey analysis revealed the levels of cooperation, communication, and critical thinking that members incorporated into their Pearls. Cooperation attributes included sharing design and learning insights, referencing other members' Pearls, referencing other members, sharing ideas, and off-line sharing. In 19% of Pearls, design insights were shared. One member described how he came up with ideas for his comic strip characters. Another 7% shared learning insights, while 13% used links to reference other Pearls. Members reported they had to be familiar with the Pearl corpus to use links. When used, however, designers reported links were a time saver.

Communication attributes included sharing personal information, asking for feedback, offering ideas, and offering opinions: 77% of Pearls included some kind of personal sharing, either in the "What I Was Thinking" section or elsewhere in the Pearl; 10% of Pearls solicited feedback from members, often asking for how-to information or asking members for alternative ways of accomplishing some design task; 21% of Pearls asked for ideas from others; and 4% of Pearls offered opinions, usually in a form that suggested their design methods were superior.

Critical thinking attributes included problem solving, design opinions, incorporation of other perspectives, meta-cognition, making connections between old and new knowledge, and innovation. Results showed that articulation of problem-solving strategies during their Clubhouse project design was seen in 18% of Pearls. Statements about what inspired the Pearl design, why the design is important, or what kind of designing the member likes to do were included in 24% of the Pearls. In 9% of Pearls, members considered or acknowledged others' points of view within the Pearl narratives. Members described how they went about thinking about problems or thinking about their Clubhouse projects in 29% of Pearls. Connections were made between old and new knowledge in 17% of the Pearls. Finally, innovative uses of Pearls were seen in 22% of the Pearls. Integration of Pearl construction with reflective thinking about projects brought Pearls directly into the heart of Clubhouse learning activities. Designers were engaged in critical reflection during an authentic design activity.

EFFECTS OF CRITICAL REFLECTION DESIGN

For most members, the initial expectation was that making Pearls would entail completing a form. When faced with the blank canvas, many expressed surprise:

> You can go through your Pearl and do whatever you like. It doesn't say
> you have to do this part first and then the next part. You can do whatever.

Many Clubhouse members associated the Pearl canvas with other software canvases they used in the past. They were accustomed to expressive freedom when using graphics programs like Photoshop and Painter, and the Pearl canvas implied a similar freedom. Members reported that writing Pearl content was "different" than writing for school:

> *Member:* I only write when I'm in school and for homework. But I don't mind so much because my Pearl ain't homework.
> *Robbin:* How is your Pearl different from homework?
> *Member:* I don't have to do it so I can write what I want and not a lot if I don't want. I like to talk about my project anyway so I don't mind.

Writing was rare in the Clubhouse and viewed by some as a nuisance or an embarrassment and a Pearl generally contains some text. A member self-conscious of his or her writing ability was taking a risk posting Pearls in such a public forum. However, designing for self-expression was a familiar activity for members: They design their Clubhouse projects. By casting reflection as a design activity, the unfamiliar problem domain was tied to a familiar activity. The Pearl canvas suggested freedom; however, members were still challenged by it. Freedom brings decisions. This provoked careful consideration of content and prompted an average of three revision cycles per Pearl. One member expressed how not only his work but his thinking would be in the public domain:

> You have to know what you're talking about because if you put it out there and you don't know what you're talking about you look stupid. I don't want to get dissed [disrespected].

These examples highlight some important aspects of this work. First, members were taking what they learned when designing their projects to inform their Pearl design processes (Perkins, 1986). Members strategically examined what was important about their project knowledge and used that to inform their Pearl designs. Also, Papert's (1980) description of learners' making new connections to old knowledge was played out during the Pearl construction process. Making Pearls engaged members in a contextual reflective activity where they were able to make new connections to their projects and their learning processes.

REVIEWING PROJECT DESIGNS IN PEARLS

Reviewing the software for their Clubhouse projects was a common part of the Pearl design process. Whether working alone or in teams, members reviewed how the project software operated. A popular technique was to open the software (e.g., Photoshop graphics software) in one window while working on the Pearl in another. In some cases, members checked additional software features not used in the original project and added those "goodies" to their Pearls. This protracted process slowed Pearl design, giving members time to think more deeply about their projects. Pearls were used to get ideas for designing other Pearls. Co-opted Pearls became a backdrop for thinking about Pearl design.

Ideas are of great interest to Clubhouse members. In particular, they wanted to know how to generate and develop new ideas. Members stored ideas for new projects and refinements in their Pearls. Those Pearls were "idea banks" for using and sharing ideas with other members. Pearls that shared ideas garnered the highest hit rates. Previously, idea sharing occurred sporadically and mostly in face-to-face encounters. Now, Pearls brought those ideas into the public domain, facilitating easier diffusion throughout the Clubhouse.

Pearls were public artifacts, which motivated designers to revisit and refine them. Most refinements involved restructuring text, attaching files, and adding images, in order to accommodate a perceived audience. Consideration of audience was a common theme when describing project experiences:

> *Member:* I explain it simpler than when I'm talking to somebody about it.
> *Robbin:* How is saying it in your Pearl different?
> *Member:* I don't know if people will know what I'm talking about. I can't look at them and see where I need to say more, so I say it real simple instead.

Here the member had a keen sense of his audience and wanted his Pearl to make sense. His solution was to break explanations into smaller, simpler pieces. He reasoned that "not being there in person" meant giving more attention to the clarity of his content. Restructuring his explanations led him to think in greater depth about his project. Another member revealed her insight that talking to someone in her Pearl was different than in person and she needed to accommodate those differences:

> *Member:* This wasn't like when somebody asks me how to do something on the computer.
> *Robbin:* What is that like?
> *Member:* I'm trying to work on my [emphasis] stuff so I want to hurry up. I just show them enough to get things going. I don't want to get stuck with them.
> *Robbin:* How is making the Pearl different?
> *Member:* Well . . . I can't go so fast. And I can't leave it looking raggedy so then I got to fix the color and make the letters bigger. Stuff like that. That takes time. Anyway, I'm working on my thing so I can take my time.
> *Robbin:* Why take the time?
> *Member:* I want to make sure it's tight. My Pearl is going to be out even if I don't finish so I got to give it a little extra flavor right then.

Members were aware others would be examining their Pearls, which motivated them to restructure content to accommodate their audience.

Clubhouse members were becoming aware of the diversity of perspectives and problem-solving techniques among their peers:

> You can get different ideas and sometimes you just get something you
> know but you don't see it right away. Then once you see how he did it
> you think, "Oh, I already know that." There's a bunch of ways to say the
> same idea.

Several members noted how they included others' Pearl design strategies into
their own:

> It was good watching Shirley do hers. I learned how she put it together,
> you know, and she didn't know what [emphasis] to put down too. You
> know what she did? She looked at her project and then she just wrote
> about the stuff she messed up before it came out right. She put in all the
> layer stuff mostly. That's what I did in mine too. I put in the clone brush
> stuff because I messed that up but then I got it. The rest was easy, but
> that was the hard part.

COLLABORATIVE PEARL REFLECTIONS

While most Clubhouse members worked on their own Pearls, on occasion two or
more members worked together. In each instance, the teams were female Clubhouse members, as one mentor noticed:

> I noticed that the girls like to work in pairs. They do that in their projects
> sometimes, so it makes sense they might make a Pearl that way.

Pearl design decisions were either negotiated or reached through turn taking.
Similar strategies were driving project design. Members took turns adding content to the Pearl. They challenged each other and reached consensus about design
features. One team talked about that experience:

> *Member:* I like making my Pearl with Carmen better.
> *Robbin:* How is it better with Carmen?
> *Member:* I guess because every time I do something I sort of ask, "What
>   do you think?" and she goes, "It's good" or she would go, "Let me
>   put that part in" or something. Sometimes it is hard to decide what
>   to put in, so we just put in some pictures. It was fun doing it with her
>   because we could talk about it.

These members had engaged in conversations that presented opportunities for
deep learning, in particular decision making and problem solving. They had developed a design strategy that included negotiation and turn taking. Clubhouse
mentors reported how Pearl teams were benefiting members:

> There is something about being on the same computer and doing it to-
> gether that makes it easier when they get confused about how to talk
> about the project. Actually, what I'm finding really interesting is how dif-

ferently Mercedes thought about her project and how her friend helped [her] thinking about it. They each had their own ideas about the best way to describe the project. All the back-and-forth was fascinating to watch. I don't remember ever hearing those kinds of exchanges in the Clubhouse before. They were really getting into the nitty-gritty details of the project and what they thought was important to talk about. If they were just talking instead of making a Pearl together it would have been more superficial.

Whether working in teams or alone, members scaffolded each other's reflections and engaged in more complex learning exchanges than generally seen in the Clubhouse.

PEARL DESIGN AS COMMUNITY PRACTICE

Over the course of the study, the design and use of Pearls became valued Clubhouse activities. Over time, language specific to Pearl design and use emerged. Members began to label Pearl design activities as *pearling*. The word *pearl* became a verb used to describe the translation of a Clubhouse project into a Pearl. Pearls also took precedence over Clubhouse projects for exhibition on Clubhouse walls. This member explained his preference for showcasing his Pearl:

> That's why I drop my Pearl. Then my name gets out there. Before, I just put up my project. How would anybody know I did it?

The term *drop* meant name-dropping, where someone's name was associated with her or his work. This was traditionally accomplished through word of mouth. However, a member's name was visible on his or her Pearl. Other members considered Pearls as a way to advertise or post an artist statement. Members seemed to prefer a richer form of public exhibition, where they got exposure for their projects and their thinking.

Over time, Pearls became a conduit for diffusion of new design tools and projects throughout the Clubhouse. Pearls on a particular topic were often preceded by Clubhouse workshops on that topic. For example, over a 2-month period and following a series of Painter workshops, seven Painter Pearls were created and after a Scratch workshop, four Scratch Pearls were created. It can be argued those Pearls were a barometer of the new software and project ideas spreading throughout the Clubhouse.

IMPLICATIONS OF PEARL USE

Pearl design requires time and effort. In some cases Pearl construction may take as much time as the original Clubhouse project. Planning, organization, refinement, and attention to audience are all vital components of the design process. That so many Pearls were made and used meant members were motivated to garner those resources necessary to produce quality Pearls. Members frequently mentioned the word "fun" to describe their Pearl design experiences. Another word that came up was "hard." One member comment was, "It's fun. It gets you a bit more into what you were doing in your project. That is kinda hard sometimes." This seemed to characterize Pearl design as what Papert called "hard fun." He argued that kids engaged in hard fun, not in spite of the fact the activity was hard but because it was hard. Such engagement was a combination of intense focus on the task at hand and intense motivation to continue.

Reflection has been described as a mechanism for transforming experience into learning and providing knowledge integration opportunities. Pearl construction situates that transformation within an authentic design practice. Reflection by design becomes a dialogue between the learner's reflective insights and the world. Constructionist learning communities like the Clubhouse are fueled by the regular practice of members designing projects and supporting another's learning. This work illustrated how building reflective artifacts and emergent reflective practice can deepen learning relationships between learners, their projects, and their peers. Those Pearl-inspired interactions occurred at several junctures: while being designed, while being used, and while being shared.

I observed that with appropriate technological and community resources youth will engage in more rigorous intellectual activities like critical reflection. The collection of Pearls, which covered a range of design tools and learning styles and strategies, became a barometer of member acuity in thinking about themselves and their work in more complex ways. The breadth and depth of the Pearl corpus conveyed how members came to view their projects through a "reflective lens." They focused attention on what helped or hindered their learning. They focused attention on how their design processes unfolded. Finally, they focused attention on how to craft their learning stories.

Design practices that typify the Clubhouse became a portal to more complex relationships between learners and their projects. An important question to consider is why members chose to build and use Pearls, when there are a myriad of software options and other activities competing for their time and attention. Members reported these reasons for using Pearls: (1) Pearls gave them a place to have their voice heard; (2) they provided a platform to broadcast their thinking and ideas, and (3) they gave them visibility within the community.

What was learned in this study is invaluable to the continued growth of learning environments like the Computer Clubhouse. Ensuring youth are engaged in deeper learning practices, such as critical reflection, is part of the Clubhouse mission. Indeed, reflective fluency characterizes a lifelong learner. It is important that we continue to examine how technology can scaffold deeper learning at both the individual and community levels.

Chapter 8

The Multiple Roles of Mentors

Yasmin Kafai, Shiv Desai,
Kylie Peppler, Grace Chiu, and Jesse Moya

Mentors play an important role in the success of every Computer Clubhouse—as in many other community organizations—and this is for multiple reasons: Mentors are there to support Clubhouse members in their projects in various ways providing technical advice, ideas, and feedback in addition to motivational support. Equally important is the tie-in to the larger community, both in local connections and professional opportunities that mentors can provide to Clubhouse members. This is why, as part of any initial charter, new Clubhouse sites are encouraged and even required to recruit and sustain ongoing mentoring partnerships with members of the local community.

While scholars and practitioners alike do not agree on one definition of *mentoring,* many base their efforts on a widely held view that mentoring involves acting as a guide, advisor, and counselor to a mentee (DuBois & Karcher, 2005; Jacobi, 1991; Monaghan & Lunt, 1992; Roberts, 2000). In recent years, this view of mentoring has come under critical review (Hart, 2006; Howard, 2006; Sullivan, 1996). In our work (Kafai, Desai, Peppler, Chiu, & Moya, 2008), we found that the Clubhouse learning model inspired a fuller range of mentoring interactions, well beyond prior top-down approaches to include more equitable, coconstructionist and learner roles for mentors. Indeed, many of the Clubhouse mentors concur that this is how the majority of their time is spent.

As we have already seen in our discussions from those in the field in Chapter 3, this is a complicated issue and filled with many unique challenges depending on the geographic location of each Clubhouse. For example, the Flagship Clubhouse's home in the Museum of Science, its connection and proximity to MIT, and its location in the Boston area, one of the nation's leading digital technology incubators, has provided the Flagship with many interested volunteers who are rich in technology expertise and also enjoy working with youth. To many, these particular circumstances may appear as serious limitations for the outreach and success of Clubhouses located in rural or other areas without access to such extraordinary human resources. In fact, while technology experience is important for mentoring in the Computer Clubhouse, it is not a necessary requirement, as our observations of mentoring in this chapter illustrate.

In the case of the Youth Opportunities Unlimited Inc. Computer Clubhouse, rather than bringing in tech-savvy engineers and programmers, undergraduate liberal arts majors with little to no extensive knowledge of computers were brought in to take on the role of Clubhouse mentors for several months. Their participation illustrates that mentoring in the Clubhouse can mean much more than just teaching and facilitating, the roles traditionally associated with mentoring. Being a mentor can also mean assuming the role of a learner, especially when working with tech-savvy Clubhouse youth. This is an important contribution to the field of research on mentoring but also speaks to those in areas without expert resources. In this chapter, we provide rich descriptions of the mentoring interactions that took place in the Youth Opportunities Unlimited Inc. Computer Clubhouse and share what mentors had to say about their mentoring experiences. Our goal is to contribute to the ongoing discussion of mentoring, which has enjoyed a veritable renaissance in corporations, universities, youth organizations, and religious and civic groups in the last decade because it is seen as addressing both career-oriented and psychosocial issues faced by disadvantaged youth from underresourced areas.

MENTORING ROLES

Before we started our observations in 2003, there were no regular mentors at the Youth Opportunities Unlimited Inc. Computer Clubhouse in South Los Angeles, with the exception of one long-term volunteer and, occasionally, graduate students from UCLA, despite the Clubhouse's repeated attempts to draw new mentors to the space. Inspired by the Fifth Dimension, which brings undergraduates into after-school programs (Cole, 2006), we decided to offer an undergraduate course in UCLA's education minor program with a community service component. As part of the course's field internship, 36 undergraduates became mentors in the Clubhouse, where they supported youth in planning, developing, and completing projects. All the participating mentors were enrolled in our seminar and field internship component. Most of them were women, with the exception of nine men, and they came from diverse ethnic backgrounds. Students were either in their third or fourth year of undergraduate study. The mentors were never formally assigned to one particular member; rather, mentors were invited to spend time in the informal environment of the Clubhouse and to feel free to take initiative with any members, as well as to make themselves available to members as needed.

All undergraduates wrote about their mentoring interactions in field notes, which over the course of 2 years created an impressive archive documenting Clubhouse activities. For this study, we collected a total of 213 field notes from the participating undergraduate mentors. We also interviewed the mentors in groups about their experiences at the end of each course. In these interviews, we used the following questions to start conversations between mentors: How did you see your role as a mentor at the beginning of the quarter? How do you see your role as a mentor now? What surprised you most in your mentoring experience? What was the hardest part about mentoring? What was the easiest? Each interview lasted about 15–20 minutes. All of the interviews were transcribed in preparation for later analyses.

THE TYPES OF MENTORING ROLES

In reviewing the field notes, we found that mentors described various interactions with members ranging from teaching to learning during the course of their field internship. This process generated various mentoring activities that we condensed in iterative rounds to five roles: teaching, facilitating, coconstructing, observing, and learning. Our goal was not to account for all recorded mentoring interactions in the field notes but to focus on those that described *sustained mentoring*. We defined sustained mentoring as any activity where a mentor was interacting with a mentee over an extended period of time (a minimum of 15–20 minutes). In the field notes either the length of the passage or the description of the amount of time that took place during the activity indicated this. We then coded all sustained mentoring interactions in field notes according to their focus: teaching, facilitating, coconstructing, observing, and learning. (For more detail, see Kafai et al., 2008). We viewed teaching at one end of the spectrum, where the mentor is directing activities, and learning at the other end of the spectrum, where youth are directing activities. In between these two extremes lie three other types of mentoring interactions: facilitating, co-constructing, and observing. This full spectrum of mentor and mentee interaction is important for developing both the leadership and knowledge base of the Clubhouse youth, or any youth for that matter.

By way of illustration, we will first describe these different mentoring roles in greater detail and provide specific examples from the undergraduate field notes. For instance, mentoring interactions that described "teaching" often listed events where the mentor dictated or controlled the majority of the content and structure of the interaction and there was evidence of intent to teach:

> I really enjoyed teaching them how to type because they were both so exited and enthusiastic about learning the correct way to type. . . . Their typing forms greatly improved, but much work still needs to be done.

> I showed him how to upload a picture of him, and then I walked him through the editing process.

> I told her to place the white arrow on the picture that she wanted to download and press the right button on the mouse and click on "Save Picture As.". . . I told her to do this for each individual picture. She had problems doing this so I had to ask her if I can use the mouse so I can show her what buttons she needed to press.

These examples showcased what is traditionally associated with mentoring—a mentor helps expand the knowledge of a Clubhouse member.

In a "facilitating" role, the mentor led the activity by providing just enough support and guidance to allow the youth to successfully explore and discover an activity at their own pace. In these situations, the mentor is still directing the learning but in a much less direct fashion. In our view, while this is similar to the type of direct instruction found in the teaching role, it differs because it allows youth to explore the problem at their own pace and provides instruction only when needed:

> I sat next to John as he used trial and error to figure the solutions to the problems. Every now and then I would give him my input.

> He chose what games he played and I just guided him through the questions and asked him things to find the solution.

> I wanted to continue to give Paulina ownership over the project, so I tried to serve as an initiator of different experiments with the program, but intentionally conceded all decision making and design choice[s] to her.

In these excerpts, the Clubhouse youth actively participated in the activity, providing input or even driving the content of the activity, but the top-down approach was much less rigid than that of a teaching role.

In "coconstructing" roles, the interaction was characterized by reciprocity between the mentor and Clubhouse youth, where neither dominated the content or character of the interaction. These activities were coconstructed, with both youth and mentor contributing and learning through the course of their interaction. There was noticeable give-and-take, resulting in a relationship within a dyad of fairly equal standing within the activity:

> We switched off controlling the mouse and tried to help each other by making suggestions. Jon would say things like, "Oh! I think I know what we need to do." I would also say similar things when he was controlling the mouse, like, "Ah, maybe you have to . . . ."

> Rosie and I experimented with the glide function. We knew where we wanted the dolphin to start and end, but we did not know the coordinates of the two places . . . . Rosie and I finally made the dolphin move the way we wanted it to.

In these excerpts, we start to see the strong role that design projects play in enabling coconstructionist learning.

When mentors take on the role of "observing," the Clubhouse youth led the content and character of the interaction but the mentor did not report that they were learning from the activity in their field notes, nor were the mentors seen as a source of information or guidance by the youth:

> I sat back while Marisol did all the work. She didn't ask for my input and I did not give it. Instead she would do something to the face and then look at me. Wait for a reaction and then move on.

> He showed me how many clams he had and was showing me the new levels he had completed (he seemed to like showing me all his accomplishments because he just showed me without me asking).

In these excerpts, we start to see that mentors can still facilitate members' involvement in Clubhouse activities by just being a supportive friend, sitting next to youth and being willing to devote time to watching their activities.

Finally, "learning" roles were interactions where the youth led the interaction with an intention to teach, and there was evidence that the mentor was learning from the interaction:

> When it failed, Alex . . . came over and showed me how to build the coaster the right way . . . . Through his help I was able to understand how you have to go about making the rollercoaster and why it only allows you to use certain pieces at certain times.

> I said, "Okay, but only if you help me because I've never done this before." (Isaac was a good teacher.) He taught me step-by-step.

> When I asked him how they were able to make movies, he said, "OK, look, I'm going to show you." He opened a new file and began to show me step- by-step how to make a movie.

When we examined all of the coded passages, we found that the most frequent type of mentoring roles were coconstructive interactions, followed by facilitating, observing, teaching, and learning (see Figure 8.1). What is most interesting about this distribution is the prevalence of mentoring interactions that place the mentor in the role of learner, observer, or coconstructor—all roles which imply a more reciprocal and equitable relationship between mentor and Clubhouse youth. These kinds of roles have been underreported in prior research on mentoring and tutoring. Teaching and facilitating are still part of the mentoring experience in the Computer Clubhouse, but they don't dominate the interactions as they would in a conventional setting.

When we further examined the distribution of roles in each student's mentoring, no undergraduates reported filling only one role, which indicated that these roles were fluid and not dependent on the types of prior experiences of the mentors. Most mentors described multiple roles of mentoring during a single visit, as the following excerpts from one mentor's field notes illustrate:

> Throughout the animation portion, Stacey and I found that he [Arnold, a Clubhouse member] was narrating the whole project . . . . Stacey and I decided that we should include a sound clip of Arnold narrating the action. . . . [The Coordinator] was able to find a microphone for Arnold to use. It was difficult to have him narrate the passage effectively since he was somewhat nervous, but after a couple of tries he was able to recall his original narrative voice. Rather than constantly give him feedback, Stacey and I let him figure out what narrative voice to use since our interference might hinder his work . . . [Coded as: Observer Role]

> After forming the basic animations and narration, we still had to figure out how to animate the soldier's beheading. Amanda became our best source as she came over and offered to help. She showed us some of her project so then we could understand how she switched head graphics.

FIGURE 8.1. Initiation of mentoring interactions by role

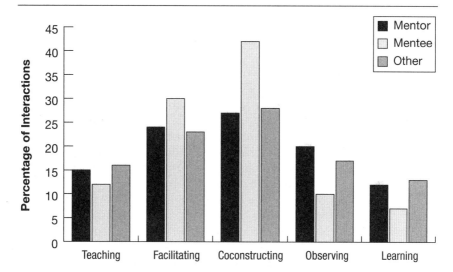

We learned from looking at Amanda's animation grid that in order to switch graphics, we had to apply a switch costumes function at the end of the previous animations for that costume . . . [Coded as: Learner Role]

Nearly one half of all mentoring interactions were initiated by mentors, compared to one third by the youth; coordinators and other mentors initiated one fifth of the interactions. This finding seems to confirm the central role that mentors play in the life of the Clubhouse in engaging and sustaining youth in activities. But these numbers also point out that Clubhouse youth sought out these contacts, and thus indicated an active stance toward requesting assistance. When we further examined the types of mentoring roles (i.e., teaching, facilitating, coconstructing, observing, or learning) that occurred in either mentor- or mentee-initiated interactions, we found that coconstructionist mentoring relationships resulted in 40% of the youth-initiated interactions (see Figure 8.1). It appears that Clubhouse members were interested in having collaborators when working on projects and those who could provide assistance (facilitator roles) or explain something when needed (teacher roles).

When we examined the context of mentoring, design activities took the lead, followed by games, socializing, and then Web surfing and homework. It should come as no surprise that design activities were most popular with coconstructive mentoring. Design activities involved the use of programming; 3-D animation; graphics software such as Scratch, Kai's SuperGoo, Bryce5, Photoshop, KidPix; game design programs such as RPG Maker; and music production software. Game activities included games on the computer, such as Roller Coaster (Tycoon), School Tycoon, video and online games, such as Whyville.net, as well as board and card games, foosball, and air hockey. Web activities involved Web surfing with youth, while homework involved mentors helping youth with anything school-related. We also created a "Personal" category to include all social activities and interactions between the mentor and youth that establish and build upon the interpersonal relationship outside of the context of other activities. In design activities, youth often invited mentors to join them in an effort to create a program, graphic design, or song and solicit their opinions about what to do in the project. The following example illustrates how design activities can provide a context for a more equitable relationship between mentor and youth:

> After we made the character's body move, I asked Jacob if he wanted to change any parts of the character. "Yes, and I want the background to be a jungle." . . . We asked [another mentor] what to do after this. She showed us how to save the picture on the server and in the Scratch folder. She labeled it "nature Jacob". We went back to the Scratch program and chose the background sprite. We then went to "load" and found "nature Jacob" and opened it. When it appeared, Jacob clapped. (We were both happy about what we were accomplishing. I had never really worked with Scratch outside of the classroom at UCLA, and the collaborative process was very exciting.) . . . We decided that we wanted the sleigh to fly. We used the glide control and the sleigh and reindeer glided, but then intersected at the top. We kept trying to figure out how to not make it do that. [The other mentor] came by and suggested that we change our x and y positions. She also helped us add sound to the reindeer that simulated bells ringing . . . . [Coded as: Coconstructor Role].

Having these types of design activities while mentoring allowed youth to have a very different relationship to adults than they might otherwise experience with homework help, games, or other types of mentoring activities.

REFLECTIONS ON MENTORING ROLES

The exit interviews provided a good opportunity to hear what mentors had to say about their preconceived ideas of going into the community as well as their reflections and experiences about mentoring in the Clubhouse. In nearly half of the interviews, mentors brought up social issues associated with the community they visited—misconceptions they had held initially about the Clubhouse members and their lack of access to resources. One of the mentors articulated this very clearly in the following passage:

> *Mentor:* [There are] a lot of preconceived notions people have going into the Clubhouse . . . . I'm not going to sit here and lie and say that I didn't already have these fed assumptions of these kids. I did take into account that I'm going to work in Inglewood and South Los Angeles. I'm thinking . . . not because they are not intellectually capable of it. It's just the things they have been exposed to [up to] this day I am assuming is limited. I was completely wrong. The first person I met was Fabian. Fabian wasn't aware of some of these things (group laughs). That idea was completely deconstructed.

> *Interviewer:* It kind of changed your notions of the area?
> *Mentor:* Yeah. The area and the kids themselves . . . . There is some
> change going [on] . . . small but there is some change. Something
> positive is going on.

Others brought up related issues about deficit notions of mentoring and what it means to need a mentor, which were also deconstructed after these experiences:

> I didn't know [anything] compared to what they knew. Usually...men-
> torship . . . is often associated . . . in a way with deficit thinking because
> they need a mentor: "They don't have this, so we are going to go in there
> and be a mentor." That's how it was associated in my brain. Once I was
> there, it was completely not like that. So that was the biggest surprise.

Three fourths of the mentors also described their multiple mentoring roles and addressed changes in their roles. Despite the benefits of being a coconstructor or learning from the members, this can be an initially uncomfortable position for the mentors who had expectations of themselves as being a tutor or Big Brother/Big Sister to the youth.

> I think [my conception of mentoring] changed from being thought of as
> being a tutor/teacher and turned into something more like a supporter/
> companion. . . . [T]he most important thing I learned in this class was
> that you don't need to pick between roles, not only playing with them
> at the green table but . . . you could be at the computers and learning
> Scratch together so . . . it was like them teaching me something and me
> teaching them something and us working together.

> I was actually surprised because I really didn't think I was going to actu-
> ally learn from the kids. When I went in, I thought, "Oh, they are going
> to have to come with me and ask me for help." But after the roles begin
> to change I was like, "OK". . . . I was really surprised.

These types of roles emerged largely due to the fact that the undergraduates had very little experience with technology outside of e-mail and cell phones. Not sur-prisingly, in nearly all the interviews, mentors reflected on their own learning and understanding about technology and often explicitly addressed their changed un-derstanding of software design or programming. Their answers might seem sur-prising given the seemingly plentiful amount of technology exposure the under-graduates have in their daily life, but few of those experiences involve the types of design technologies found in the Clubhouse. This demonstrates the powerful effect that the Clubhouse has, not only on its members but on its mentors as well.

Our findings clearly demonstrate that mentoring in the Clubhouse comprises different interactions, ranging from teaching to learning, which is an unusual ex-perience for volunteers working with youth in the after-school hours. One surpris-ing finding in the field notes was the strong presence of coconstructive interactions that put mentors and Clubhouse youth on more equal footing. It is possible that the constructionist nature (Kafai, 2006) of the Clubhouse played a role in this finding, which placed an emphasis on design activities over games and Web surfing. We know that nearly one quarter of all reported mentoring interactions focused on design activities and these might be more conducive to a collaborative effort.

MENTORING PARTNERSHIPS

We want to take our expanded notion of mentoring a step further and suggest thinking about Clubhouse mentoring as a form of partnership. Such a mentoring partnership is built on the assumption that college youth, who often have unprecedented access to technology use in their daily lives and schooling, might be well positioned to work on technology projects with urban youth from underserved communities often described as the primary victims of the Digital Divide (Warschauer, 2004). Yet when faced with design technologies, most undergraduates, especially those from the liberal arts, have little experience beyond Web browsing and game playing and thus find themselves in situations where they become learners of new creative technologies (Goode, 2004). For these reasons, mentoring partnerships offer the possibility of a more equitable and reciprocal relationship that opposes the deficit perspective prevalent in many mentoring efforts (Villalpando & Solorzano, 2005). This perspective assumes that mentors are the providers of advice and holders of knowledge found lacking in mentees.

In a review of the literature, prior discussions of the learning benefits of mentoring have addressed aspects such as civic participation, improved self-esteem, and increased opportunities to interact with peers different from themselves, but these benefits were seen as outcomes and not as features of the mentoring process itself. Learning roles were overwhelmingly associated with design activities at the Computer Clubhouse. This finding may be of interest to other programs wanting to stimulate a full range of mentoring roles in informal settings.

One of the reasons why we think this approach might work well in Clubhouse settings is because mentors are modeling how to learn for the members. They are modeling what questions to ask when you don't know something, what resources to draw upon when you want to solve a problem, and how to effectively listen to someone else. This also provides the mentors an opportunity to showcase and articulate their understanding, deepening the learning experience for the members. In effect, this approach is all about modeling how to learn about learning—a much more complicated approach to teach than the ins and outs of various technical skill sets. This is due in part because technology itself is ever changing, which provides a perfect context for this type of mentoring model. The design projects also enabled mentors with multiple types of backgrounds to enter into these experiences, something that wouldn't be possible with narrowly technical activities lacking the media-rich aspects of the tools and software available at the Clubhouse.

The implications from studying mentoring at the Computer Clubhouse present several promising directions for mentoring and community service learning in general (Vogelsang & Astin, 2000). To conceptualize mentoring as learning opportunities for academic skills challenges core assumptions of who can be a mentor and for whom. For fields such as computer science, there is an assumption that technical skills are a necessary qualification for becoming a mentor. Our findings suggest that it is a possible, but not a necessary, prerequisite. The idea of having mentors learn along with youth offers a promising venue to rethink what we mean by mentoring. Such a mentoring partnerships model would also be possible to replicate with other types of community partners and need not be a university partner, which would be more amenable to sites seeking mentoring support in areas without universities in the close vicinity.

Chapter 9

The Computer Clubhouse Village: Sharing Ideas and Connecting Communities of Designers Across Borders

Elisabeth Sylvan

While the Computer Clubhouse started in one city, over the last 15 years it has grown into an international network with over 100 Clubhouses worldwide (see Chapter 2). Supporting this global community and providing flexibility for local coordinators to organize their Clubhouses has provided a challenge—and an opportunity—for the Computer Clubhouse Network staff. The design of its intranet site, called the "Computer Clubhouse Village" or "Village" for short, supports the independence of individual Clubhouses, while maintaining organization and encouraging the flow of communication throughout the Clubhouse Network.

In the Village members join the worldwide Clubhouse community to share creations, connect with their peers, and have their voices heard. Members can post their work, leave comments on others' and indicate they like a project by marking it with a "cool ping." They create highly personalized profile pages with photos, music, and videos. They have a forum for discussing issues important to them. Through the Village, Clubhouse members can get involved with new projects and interact with others outside their Clubhouse in ways unimaginable without it.

The Village also supports the Clubhouse staff and mentors organizing across the disparate, independently functioning physical Clubhouses. It provides an area for mentors to share tools and tips for better scaffolding of member activities (see Chapter 8). In addition, there are mechanisms for staff to manage activities and document processes, which can often be accomplished faster and more efficiently online. The ability to pool lessons learned and exchange ideas is of critical importance, given the scale and diversity of the organization.

In contrast with many current social networking sites like Facebook or My-Space, Village membership is restricted to members, mentors, and staff of the over 100 Computer Clubhouses worldwide. It is important that the Village provides a safe online environment and ensures only Clubhouse community members have access. Every account on the Village represents a member of the global Clubhouse community and only Clubhouse staff can create new accounts. That ensures that every account holder is known personally. Members can safely share personal information, post their photographs, and participate in synchronous, real-time chat or asynchronous threaded discussion postings and e-mails. Many youth at the Clubhouse feel strongly that the Village belongs to them and they may express their grief or troubles in that forum in ways they may not do in person. If a member drastically alters his or her online identity, steals other people's work, or acts out, someone at the local Clubhouse knows the member personally. When issues arise, Clubhouse staff or mentors can intervene face-to-face in culturally appropriate ways.

The Village is composed of five main sections (Figure 9.1). The "Projects" section includes all the projects people have shared, along with "Things to Try" and "Galleries." The "People & Clubhouses" section features a home page for each Clubhouse along with links to photo albums and profiles. From their profile pages, Villagers can post photo albums and galleries, create personal profiles, and e-mail one another. The "Software Studio" section lists all the software available at the Clubhouses, along with help references and links. The "Talk" section contains various discussion groups and chat capabilities. The "Topic Tree" section is an editable repository of Clubhouse-related information. It includes information on various Clubhouse issues such as sustainability, tutorials, digital photography, Web design, and gender equity. Village menus are available in many languages and additional content has been either posted in or translated to Spanish. However, the majority of Village content is delivered in English.

TYPES OF ACTIVITIES ON THE VILLAGE

Overall there are three areas of member activity on the Village intranet site. In the first area members create an online presence or representation of themselves, while in the second area they share projects and project-related information. In the third area members socialize and discuss issues important to them.

Online Presence

Villagers define their online presence and explore others through a variety of mechanisms. The map of Clubhouses across the globe emphasizes the range of cultures represented. This page rotates through featured Villagers' profiles, giving a sense of the diversity of the Village community. Individual profile pages contain personal photos albums, project galleries, and descriptions of who they are. For instance, one boy from the Philippines talked about the friends he had made and what he loved to do at the Clubhouse:

> huhhh . . . . i really missed those people who makes me laugh at the summit . . . . i will treasure the moments we've shared . . . . i really miss you . . . . muahhh hi guyz i'm frank . . . . from the beautiful, amazing place called philippines . . . . I really love ny friends (just check out my album and you'll see our pictures) they are good friends . . . . i'm 15 yrs old. . .

FIGURE 9.1. Screenshot of Computer Clubhouse Village

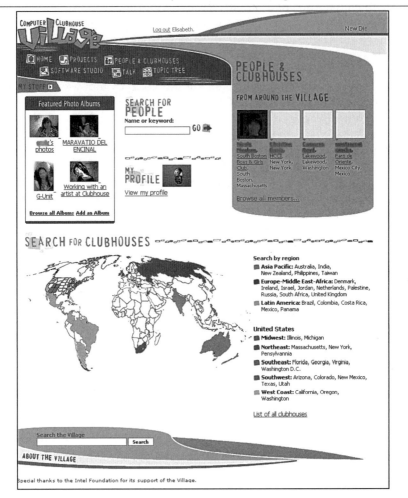

I love—photoshop because I can express my creativity through editing pictures—hanging out with my friends—going to the clubhouse to mingle with other members—Philippines I'm funny friendly person.

Many profiles are detailed representations of what the members do, who their friends are, what music they like, and what they create at the Clubhouse. Some profiles include photographs of themselves, their family, and friends, or pictures of animals, music stars, and sports stars they like. Active members update their background information regularly. Others add music videos, sometimes running multiple videos at once, creating a cacophony on their pages. Members use their profile pages to broadcast interest in connecting with others or connections they already have made. The Clubhouse and Village are designed to empower members' voices. That speaks directly to an important component of the Clubhouse experience, which is youth not just being connected but also being heard.

Project Sharing

The "Projects" area is a dynamic one, where different work is featured regularly and contributions are added. Most notable is how members use the projects to express their passions and concerns (see color plates at end of Part II). The project content is informed by the members' interests, which might reflect personal preferences, such as favorite food, music, or anime. Their projects also may illustrate what they see in their worlds, such as cars, graffiti, sunsets, or the desert. Many projects convey what is fashionable in the world of youth, and especially teens. Pop musicians and their music are frequently sources of inspiration, as are sports personalities. Other projects may be created with tools such as Blender (3-D models), Lego Mindstorms (robotics), GameMaker (game design), and music composition using the ever-popular music studio.

Socializing and Discussing Issues

In addition, Clubhouse members spend much of their time on the Village connecting through e-mail, discussion groups, and monitored chat sessions. Some topics are guided by administrators, such as help with the Village, multilingual support, and staff sections. Others are set up for villagers around topics that interest them. One of the most popular discussion areas, "Clubhouse Talk," is dedicated to chatting about everything from Dance Dance Revolution (a video game which involves dancing) and Krumping (see Chapter 6) to favorite sports and foods to Ramadan. The individual posts often reflect what members care about and wish to share about themselves. The larger topic threads illustrate youths' understanding of the diversity of their community and their desire to communicate with one another:

> *Member 1:* If you could go anywhere in the world, where would you go and why?
> *Member 2:* . . . there's two places i would go to: Japan and any beach in the world. I want to go to Japan because they make all the things I like such as anime and video games! I would also want to go to a beach because I really want to swim in the ocean.
> *Member 3:* . . . love ya [Member 2]! but i would go to rome and amsterdam!! rome because i want to see the leaning tower of pisa, and amsterdan because i like the movie Deuce bigalo Part 2!

This exchange not only reflects these particular Clubhouse members' dreams, but also the global nature of the Village. Members are interested in connecting with their peers and how their peers perceive them. This builds a stronger community that is a comfortable place to share one's creations.

HOW THE CLUBHOUSE COMMUNITY USES THE VILLAGE

As of April 2007 the Village community was composed of over 6,000 participants, including over 5,000 active youth members, over 400 mentors, over 150 coordinators and assistant coordinators, and various other staff. Over 63% of the youth members were from the United States, 6% were from the Philippines, 4% each from Columbia, Mexico, and Northern Ireland, along with members from the remaining Clubhouses worldwide. Village participants were representative of the larger Clubhouse community (see also Chapter 10): The average age was 15 and 50% of members were female. About 75% described their primary language as English, 17% as Spanish, 2% as Filipino, and the remaining other languages included Chinese, Danish, Dutch, German, Hebrew, Hindi, Kannada, Portuguese, and Russian.

Although members use all sections of the Village, they engaged in some activities more frequently than others. By far the most popular section was e-mail, accounting for about half of all page hits. That was not surprising given the community consists primarily of adolescents who are likely interested in connecting with other adolescents. The next most popular activity was viewing members' profile pages, which accounts for 15% of page hits. Additionally youth spend on average about 2 minutes on each profile page, which suggests they were examining the content of those pages. Members developed profile pages to be noticed, and it appears that was happening.

Other Village sections receive fewer hits, but visitors stay for up to 2 minutes on those pages suggesting that the page content was being more thoroughly examined. Those pages included the "Home Page"—which displayed a variety of rotating content and provided a snapshot of what's happening on the Village; "Things to Try"—which provided project ideas; and "Software Studio" and the "Profile Survey"—both of which support online, interactive activities.

E-MAIL ON THE VILLAGE

E-mail, as noted earlier, is by the far the most popular activity on the Village. It is the primary mechanism for members to communicate privately. In the 31 months of e-mail studied, 83% of Villagers e-mailed at least once. Villagers sent, on average, 100 e-mails per person with a median of 3. The distribution of number of e-mails sent is logarithmic, which means that most users sent very few e-mails while a handful sent a lot. Adults working at the Clubhouse have noted that members who use e-mail frequently have short, rapid interactions in the style of instant messaging. When Clubhouse members used the e-mail application, the primary activity was checking to see what messages had arrived. The next most popular activity was actually reading the content of messages, and the least popular was sending e-mail. One might expect that users flip back and forth rapidly between their e-mail boxes and other activities. In fact, people spent as much time looking at their e-mail boxes as they spent on pages for sending e-mail.

A study of the e-mail exchanges among Village members reveals that members use e-mail to connect with people they wouldn't otherwise know (Sylvan, 2007). For instance, though Villagers connect with people within their own Clubhouse, most e-mail connections were made between members in different Clubhouses. Most likely, these members had never meet in person and formed connections via the Village. When Villagers do connect with people within their Clubhouse, these exchanges are less frequent and composed of fewer e-mails. These findings suggest that Village is succeeding in building relationships across the Computer Clubhouse Network. Still, there were fewer connections between Clubhouses in different countries than between Clubhouses within the same country. This may reflect the impact of different languages and cultures between countries in prohibiting some connections.

UNDERSTANDING PARTICIPATION ON THE VILLAGE

Clubhouse coordinators and Network staff have been concerned about what members do on the Village. A statistical analysis revealed that male-female communication was significantly more common than same gender communication. Also, male-female connections were found to have stronger ties than same gender connections (Sylvan, 2007). While the designers of the Village and Clubhouse coordinators wanted members to connect with one another and socialize, they were also concerned that the Village could devolve into a "dating site" like the popular MySpace.com. The Village was designed to connect members and support an exchange of their design projects and ideas. In the following excerpt from a chat-based meeting, Clubhouse coordinators summarize the issues around member e-mailing versus being engaged in other Village activities:

> *Coordinator 1:* The Village is a channel for them to interchange ideas.
> *Coordinator 2:* We have to limit the time on Village and we try to motivate them to upload problems and get news from network. I think it's OK.
> *Coordinator 3:* On the contrary, I think it's good because they can contribute diverse visions. But I don't see it as a problem. It's much better if they establish safe relationships within the network as opposed to on MySpace.
> *Coordinator 4:* The Village is a valuable resource but we have to focus it positively.

So are members primarily socializing or are they engaged in project-related exchanges? To answer this question, various online activities were examined, including the number of e-mails sent, Village web sites visits, profile page updates, and project postings (Sylvan, 2007). A statistical test revealed that people who e-mailed often also visited the Village significantly more often than those who e-mailed infrequently. A second test revealed that those members sending frequent e-mails also updated their profile pages more often, as well.

Posting projects is an important way members contribute to the Village. Uploading is a multistep process that requires more effort than e-mailing or other online discussion activities. Also, members need to feel confident that they have a project they wish to share. Despite these challenges, 26% of all Clubhouse Village members upload their projects to the Village area.

More importantly, people who e-mailed the most post significantly more projects than those who sent fewer e-mails.This finding addresses the concern that members are using the Village for purely social reasons. Of course, it still is possible and, perhaps likely, that e-mail could be used to meet potential boyfriends or girlfriends online. However, that kind of activity does not appear to be occurring at the expense of the design goals of the Village. Members who participated in one way (via e-mail) participated in other ways as well.

What these findings suggest is that though there was a wide range of e-mail usage, Clubhouse members who e-mailed often did not do so at the expense of other Village-related activities. Instead, they e-mailed in addition to other activities. It appears Clubhouse youth, concerned about who they are and how they fit in, use their projects, profiles, discussion groups, and other forms of text communication to reach out to others.

DIFFUSION OF A NEW VILLAGE FEATURE

A way to encourage productive member connections was to augment those activities members already engage in on the Village. As mentioned previously, a core member activity on the Village was visiting profile pages. The "Village Profile Survey" was created to augment members' existing interest in designing their profile pages and surfing other members' pages. The "Village Profile Survey" is not a standardized survey instrument but rather an informal questionnaire that members fill out and put on their profile pages. The survey was composed of 19 questions, including who you are, what you like, what you do at the Clubhouse, and what technologies you use. The survey was first launched on the Village home page, but 88% of Village users completed the survey after finding it on other members' profile pages. This survey also enabled the tracking of how ideas diffused through the Village by examining the frequency of e-mails and page hits on profiles. We found that members who have logged on to the Village more frequently also tended to adopt the survey earlier (Sylvan, 2007).

In a further step, we analyzed relationships among answers Villagers gave to the survey. The largest cluster of answers involved responses about technologies, which is appropriate for the Village community. For example, Photoshop is popular at the Clubhouse and was commonly cited. The technology words were associated with other words such as *fun, people, game,* and *projects.* This implied those words are associated with social and fun activities by the Villagers. These results are promising because the survey was designed to encourage members to relate to one another as project creators and potential collaborators. Location-related words were also common, suggesting members liked to discuss where they were from and where they would like to visit. Again, this was encouraging because it suggested members may be finding commonalities, both locally and from across the globe.

DESIGN DECISIONS ABOUT THE VILLAGE

When designing and participating in communities for youth, we are faced with challenging design choices. Youth want to socialize with their peers, and it is important for their development that they do so. But online sites that solely provide ways to socialize may lack content that can deepen interactions and create meaningful connections. On the other hand, a site that is too centrally controlled, both in content and expressive freedom, may not be interesting to this age group. The Village designers have achieved a balance between the dynamic and open nature of the Computer Clubhouse community by providing a safe, supportive online environment where youth can interact. Computer Clubhouse Village development remains a fluid process of participating in the community, observing what happens, anticipating needs, and adapting.

On the Village all members' accounts are created by an adult who knows them. Since every member is known personally by someone at his or her local Clubhouse, mentors and staff who monitor the site can note when someone is struggling or being hurtful. Should problems arise, someone from the local Clubhouse can talk one-on-one with that member to resolve the issue. Youth being seen and heard is part of the Clubhouse culture. Furthermore, the Village not only provides a mechanism for having a voice, it also provides models of how to use that voice constructively. By actively and enthusiastically participating on the site, adults and mentors model what it means to engage constructively in an online community of creators. If members see the richness that comes from people participating civilly and thoughtfully, they will be more likely to do the same. Sites like the Village give youth an opportunity to practice responsible citizenship in online communities.

It is important to note that the Village was not simply created and released to its audience. Designers watched how youth used it, asked them what did and did not work, and tweaked and redesigned over the years. For instance, the first installment of the Village did not have a chat function. However, it became clear members were interested in chatting online. Once the chat feature was introduced, chat sessions had a specified topic that was monitored by staff or the Village design team. Developers of online communities for youth, such as the Village, have to anticipate and adapt to its members' expectations. Designing the Village was an ongoing process of participation, study, and trial and error.

CONCLUSIONS

The Computer Clubhouse Village is an intranet site designed to connect and empower the youth of the Clubhouse. The site supports the Clubhouse Guiding Principle that speaks to learner empowerment through the creative and socially supported uses of technology. The Clubhouse community comes to the Village to learn about technology and to share ways of using it and creating with it. The Village also provides a window from individual Clubhouses into the global Clubhouse community. It exposes youth to a larger worldview than in their local Clubhouses and neighborhoods. Members find inspiration from peers from different backgrounds and cultures and countries who are passionate about creating with technology. Youth share their different experiences and discover common ground and inspiration.

On this site members of the Clubhouse community can share projects and ideas, discuss issues important to them, and get to know one another. Members use the site to connect with others they would not otherwise be able to connect with. Still, the social connections that the members made do not come at the expense of them sharing and discussing their work. Members who connect with peers from around the world also go to the site more, update their profiles more often, and post more projects. These connections to new people and new ideas expose members to a wider view of the world around them.

PART IV

SHOWCASES OF COMPUTER CLUBHOUSE SUCCESSES

I N THIS FINAL PART, we focus our attention on the outcomes and impact of the Clubhouse learning model. As Gail Breslow, the director of the Computer Clubhouse Network and author of the first chapter in this part states, "Defining and assessing the participation, engagement, and impact of the Clubhouse program on young people's lives has been a challenge and a learning experience for the entire Clubhouse community over the past 15 years." She presents key features of the Clubhouse model and findings about members' participation, technology expertise, and confidence that have been captured by several independent evaluators. The chapter outlines different approaches for assessment in Computer Clubhouses that not only document impact but also provide data for informed change.

Chapter 11, written by Brenda Abanavas and Robbin Chapman, illustrates how information gathered about the network can provide impetus for programmatic change. The Hear Our Voices project addressed the lack of participation of girls in Clubhouse activities observed at several sites. This finding mirrors the well-documented absence of women and minorities in the technology industry and culture at large. The Clubhouse organization initiated a program in 20 Clubhouses that reserved one day in the week for girls only, providing them with access to technology resources, female mentors and role models, a community of peers, and a positive learning environment. The lessons learned from this intervention have shown impact at the network level.

In Chapter 12, Yasmin Kafai, Kylie Peppler, Grace Chiu, John Maloney, Natalie Rusk, and Mitchel Resnick turn our attention to one particular aspect of technology fluency: programming. This was expected to be present from the beginning but turned out to be mostly absent in the activities of many Clubhouses. Our evaluation focuses on 2 years of observation in one Computer Clubhouse where programming had initially not taken root. We then examine various normative, political, and technical aspects that contributed to the change, among them the introduction of a new programming environment oriented toward media production, an increased amount of mentor support, and a university-community partnership.

Clearly, the findings reported in this section provide selected views on a complex learning infrastructure that involves over 100 Clubhouses on five continents. While each Clubhouse shares a commitment to the four principles, each also provides an example of adaptation to local circumstances. That this has been possible at all is perhaps the most important outcome and deserves further examination in the long run. But in this book our goals were to provide evidence in multiple forms that Clubhouse learning is a viable and crucial enterprise for today's youth.

Chapter 10

Participation, Engagement, and Youth Impact in the Clubhouse Network

Gail Breslow

In the mid-1990s, community technology centers opened in many low-income neighborhoods around the country with an eye toward addressing what eventually became known as the Digital Divide. And yet many struggled to find ways to attract youth on a sustained basis, or did so by offering free access to the Internet or by stocking their centers with computer games and other entertainment. In contrast, community leaders would visit the Computer Clubhouse and marvel at the fact that young people chose of their own accord, day in and day out, to come to a place where game playing was not allowed and the Internet was a tool not for passive browsing but for finding inspiration to express their own ideas and then communicate them to the rest of the world.

From the early days of the first Computer Clubhouse at the Computer Museum, it was evident that the Clubhouse was not just about providing access to technology. Interest in the Computer Clubhouse—in what makes it work and in how to go about starting one in other underserved neighborhoods—came from many sources: community leaders, youth service providers, and educational researchers. But with growing interest in the Clubhouse came unanswered questions and challenges. Many visitors would ask for a list of the software we were utilizing, as though Photoshop or Director in some way was the magic ingredient that made the Clubhouse successful. Others would ask for our hardware specs, or want to take photographs of the physical layout of the Clubhouse. While all those aspects of the Clubhouse certainly played a role in its early success, they were not the "secret sauce" (as one of our early supporters at Intel dubbed it) that made the Clubhouse uniquely effective. It became apparent that framing the relevant questions—and supporting the right qualities in organizations that wanted to start Computer Clubhouses—would be essential to extend the reach and impact of the program around the world.

Back in 1995 there was only one Computer Clubhouse, tucked in on the waterfront edge of Boston's urban neighborhoods, still in its infancy. But many community leaders and youth service providers had visited the Clubhouse, met Clubhouse youth, and seen its potential to deeply affect the lives of young people who might not otherwise find a place to express their ideas, not to mention experience the joy of learning and pride of creating (and showing off) their projects. When the position of director of the Computer Clubhouse program was first established in 1995, the goal was clear: to determine how best to fulfill the Clubhouse's potential to change lives and transform communities, both in Boston and beyond. But defining and capturing the participation, engagement, and impact of the Clubhouse program on young people's lives has been a challenge and a learning experience for the entire Clubhouse community over the past 15 years.

This chapter describes different approaches to Clubhouse assessment that have been utilized over the years to track participation, document impact, and—perhaps most important—provide input for informed change. In addition to analyzing more than a decade's worth of sign-in data and assessment and planning reports conducted twice a year by each Clubhouse, over the past 10 years the Clubhouse Network has drawn on the work of two independent research and evaluation firms: Education Development Center's Center for Children and Technology and, more recently, SRI International's Center for Technology in Learning. In particular, SRI's research from 2003–2008, commissioned by the Museum of Science with funding from the Intel Foundation, provides a range of insights related to Clubhouse youth participation and the attitudes, beliefs, and aspirations associated with participation.

PARTICIPATION AS EMPOWERMENT

Although the Clubhouse founders believed strongly in the importance of evaluation, only a few assessment processes were put in place in the early days of the Clubhouse. A simple paper survey of the first participants back in 1993 showed that 70% had never used a mouse before, but the most meaningful long-term evaluation tool was a very different one: a sign-in system to capture information about who was coming, how often, and for how long. While it might have been rudimentary, it has provided an important source of data not only about participation over the years but also about impact. Clubhouse participation data showed—and continues to show—high percentages of teens "voting with their feet" to come to the Computer Clubhouse, making a positive and active choice about how to spend their time. While many after-school programs face challenges attracting and retaining teen participants, the Clubhouse's inherent focus on self-motivated activity, its underlying message of respect and responsibility, and the validation of young people's personal interests and passions appeal to teens confronted with possible choices for how they spend their out-of-school time. As one community leader making his first visit to the Clubhouse put it, as he surveyed a room teeming with animated young people actively engaged in projects of their own making: "This isn't a computer program, this is a youth empowerment program!"

TABLE 10.1. Average Clubhouse Participation Across 94 Clubhouses (July—December 2007)

During this time period	Average	Median	Standard Deviation	Normalized Average
Daily average # members	40	25	49.55	29
Daily average % girls	40	44	16.34	42
Daily average % teens	53	50	26.15	53
At the end of the period:				
Total # active Members	243	170	251.53	160

Note: From Computer Clubhouse self-assessment and planning reports.

An Active Membership

Today the Clubhouse serves roughly 25,000 youth in over 100 Clubhouses in 21 countries around the world. On average each Clubhouse sees about 250 youth per year, but most youth participate several times a week and stay involved for an extended period of time over many years, often returning as alumni to volunteer or work on staff. Table 10.1 shows average participation across 94 Clubhouses during a typical 6-month period. As seen, most Clubhouses saw a high daily percentage of teens ages 13–18 (53%) during this time period, and slightly lower participation of girls (42% girl visits on average).

Findings from a recent SRI International survey of Clubhouse youth (Gallagher & Michalchik, 2007) show that members' level of commitment to the Clubhouse is quite high: Of 1,180 youth respondents from 55 Clubhouses, an average of 51% of Clubhouse members claimed to visit their Clubhouse every day, and as many as 85% said they visited their Clubhouse at least weekly. Not only did they visit frequently, but they also stayed for extended periods of time: 80% reported staying for at least one hour. About one third (31% of girls and 39% of boys) said they stayed for more than 3 hours during a typical visit.

What Clubhouse Members Do

Even more impressive is how Clubhouse members spend their time. In the same survey, nearly 90% of members reported usually participating in at least one of the activities, such as making a design or picture; making a video or animation; making something in the music studio; or creating a game, toy, or robot (see Figure 10.1).

SRI's study found only two activities where there is more than a 10 percentage point difference between boys and girls: more boys reported making a video or animation whereas more girls reported writing a newsletter, article, or story.

FIGURE 10.1. Percentage of Clubhouse members participating in each activity, by gender

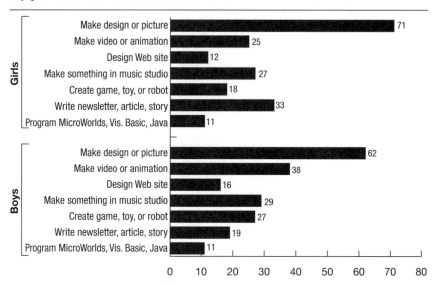

Note: Of 495 girls, 685 boys responding, "usually participating in this activity." From the May 2007 Youth Impact Survey, published by SRI International.

Participation by Gender: An Opportunity

Simply understanding the demographics of Clubhouse participants—not only age but also gender, neighborhood of residence (as a proxy for household income and makeup), ethnicity, grade level, and school—goes a long way toward helping us begin to understand the Clubhouse's potential impact on young people's lives, as well as how to enhance that impact. For example, statistics from the early days of the Clubhouse showed that less than 30% of registered Clubhouse members were girls and that girls participated much less often than boys. While not surprising in light of societal influences on girls and technology, as well as the more limited mobility of girls in urban neighborhoods (Margolis & Fisher, 2003), this finding gave us the motivation—and the basis to seek funding—to establish a girls' only program at the Clubhouse (see Chapter 11). The focus is not only on creating a safe space for girls to explore their own ideas through technology without the presence of boys as either distraction or domination, but also providing female staff and adult mentors as role models to ensure that girls find ways to express themselves that are personally relevant and meaningful to them.

Although Clubhouses still need to pay attention to the gender mix of participation in their programs—especially given cultural biases against girls and technology in many communities around the world—statistics show that girls represent 42% of Clubhouse participants across all Clubhouses in 2008, and attend in roughly equal frequencies as boys. In fact, in light of trends in the United States and elsewhere of boys graduating high school in fewer numbers than girls and more often confronted with negative influences such as gangs and drugs, many Clubhouses have started male-only programs to ensure that boys are supported in the Clubhouse in ways that uniquely enable them to understand their own potential and how to realize that potential.

BEYOND PARTICIPATION: ACTIVE ENGAGEMENT

As interest in the Clubhouse learning model began to grow—spurred by replication of the Clubhouse program at the Boys and Girls Clubs of Boston, the Museo de los Niños in Bogotá, and elsewhere—it became obvious that our focus on participation data was not sufficient. Although it was clear the Clubhouse was having a life-changing effect on many young people's lives, the budding Computer Clubhouse Network needed information about and evidence of impact in order to inspire funders and community leaders to make substantial investments in support of a program that was unique and unproven. But the challenges of measuring the effects of a drop-in program—where youth come and go as they please—and capturing impacts that aspire far beyond just providing access to technology were daunting. In 2000, when Intel signed on to support the Clubhouse Network with a commitment to 100 Clubhouses around the world, a formative evaluation identified five kinds of youth outcomes in the following areas (Pryor, McMillan, Lutz, & John, 2001):

- Technological fluency: the ability to express oneself through technology
- Collaboration: the ability to collaborate, communicate, and work in teams
- Problem solving: the ability to solve complex problems
- Planning: the ability to develop, plan, and execute complex projects
- Confidence: developing self-esteem and self-confidence

But a reluctance to conduct participant surveys, which would take young people away from their activities and potentially feel invasive, left us struggling for how best to capture these outcomes, if not through case studies or in-depth qualitative research over time (a prohibitively expensive option at the time). As a result, evaluation efforts focused on the factors that contribute to a Clubhouse's success and on the development of tools to help young people reflect on their own experience, both being important contributions in the evolution of our understanding of the important qualities of the Clubhouse learning model and how best to measure youth outcomes (Pasnik & Meade, 2003).

In fact, this formative evaluation work on the factors that contribute to a Clubhouse's success informed our development of a comprehensive assessment and planning tool that provides Clubhouse coordinators and their managers with a means to evaluate and reflect on the quality of their own Clubhouse program and to address any issues or challenges they may face. Twice a year, every Clubhouse in the network evaluates the various components that contribute to Clubhouse success, including Clubhouse goals and the learning model, youth programming in the Clubhouse, staff and volunteer skills, training and development, organization support, and financial administration and planning. For examples, consult the *Computer Clubhouse Impact Around the World* page (Evaluation link from About Us) at the Computer Clubhouse Network Web site (http://www.computerclubhouse.org/reports.htm).

In turn, each component is broken down into individual characteristics that contribute to Clubhouse practice. For example, Clubhouse goals and the learning model include:

- Encouraging young people to work as designers, inventors, and creators and helping them learn to express themselves with technology
- Encouraging youth to work on projects related to their own interests
- Helping members acquire skills in problem solving and executing complex projects
- Creating a sense of community and encouraging teamwork and collaboration
- Offering resources and opportunities to those who would not otherwise have access to them, in an environment of trust and respect

Clubhouse staff is encouraged to identify areas of improvement and to define steps that they plan to take and resources they require to address those areas. The assessment serves as much as a vehicle for reflection and discussion between Clubhouse coordinators and their local management as it does as a resource for the network. Yet it provides important insights for the Clubhouse Network in aggregate, illuminating issues and challenges that Clubhouses are commonly facing around the world.

For example, in 2004 over 40% of Clubhouses reported that linking Clubhouse interests to college and career exploration was an area in which they would like to improve. The Clubhouse Network responded by increasing resources and attention to this area, drawing on Intel Foundation funding to provide Clubhouse-to-College/Clubhouse-to-Career (C2C) minigrants for Clubhouses that proposed innovative approaches to raising the bar, and raising visibility of the C2C College Scholarships offered by the Clubhouse Network. Two years later, Clubhouses reported a much higher satisfaction level with the level of college and career awareness and youth leadership opportunities ("Members take part in youth leadership opportunities") in their individual Clubhouses (see Figure 10.2).

As rich and meaningful as the participation data and results from the assessment and planning process might be, the question still remained: What is the impact of Clubhouse participation on youth, in terms of their social and emotional attitudes, academic attitudes, technology use, and aspirations for the future? As part of ongoing evaluation work with the Intel Computer Clubhouse Network, SRI designed a Youth Impact Survey, administered six times between February 2005 and May 2007 via the World Wide Web and in paper format to all Clubhouses. This survey solicited information about members' background and Clubhouse visiting patterns. The survey also included scales that measured attitudes and behaviors that SRI and the Clubhouse Network identified as expected outcomes of members' Clubhouse participation.

FIGURE 10.2. Computer Clubhouse self-assessment, 2004 vs. 2006

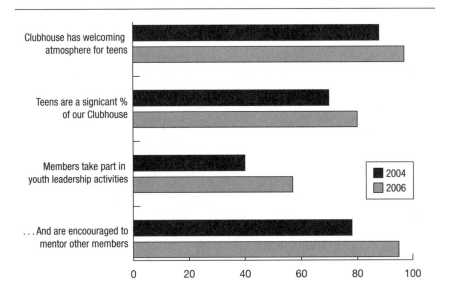

Note: During the period July–December 2004 (79 Clubhouses reporting) and July–December 2006 (96 Clubhouses reporting). From Computer Clubhouses self-assessment and planning reports.

A total of 3,732 different members participated in at least one survey, with 750 of these members (20%) participating in at least two surveys. Furthermore, 92 Clubhouses participated in at least one survey. To develop the survey, SRI researchers collaborated with Network staff, starting in early 2004, to determine the types of outcomes that would best align with learning opportunities available to Clubhouse members. SRI reviewed hundreds of pages of documentation from individual Clubhouses on the types of impacts they were seeing. Additionally, SRI visited Clubhouses throughout the state of California in the development phase of the survey, piloting it with approximately 200 members. SRI researchers also visited Clubhouses in subsequent phases of survey development and administration to discuss coordinators' views on the impacts of the Clubhouse.

The survey was administered twice a year for the first three years, but we concluded that there was insufficient insight gained from this and reduced the frequency both as a cost- and time-saving measure and also to minimize the surveying of youth who are frequently subjected to standardized testing and measurement. In the spirit of the Clubhouse as a place to express one's own voice and contribute to the greater Clubhouse community, however, Clubhouse youth are encouraged to think of the youth impact survey as a time when they can express their own views about who they are, how they feel, and how they have changed. In addition, youth are encouraged to think of the survey as a responsibility of Clubhouse membership, as voting in an election would be an act of responsible citizenship.

In 2008, the 15th anniversary year of the Clubhouse program, a qualitative study drawing on the large body of documentation gathered over several years by the Clubhouse Network was added to the quantitative assessments of the impact of Clubhouse participation, supplemented with site visits to Clubhouses and interviews with Clubhouse staff from around the world (Michalchik, Llorente, & Lundh, 2008). The findings show three broad types of behavioral outcomes for Clubhouse members: their use of twenty-first-century skills, including technological fluency; their capacity to follow pathways to success; and their commitment to community and service.

Whereas technology use is widely viewed as one of the core skills necessary in the twenty-first-century workplace, the assessments point to the ways in which the Clubhouse environment provides young people opportunities to develop other twenty-first-century skills as well, such as problem-solving skills, creativity, communication skills, and the ability to work well with others (see Figures 10.3 and 10.4). One of the more compelling findings from the youth impact surveys is the correlation between many of these skills and the relative time spent in the Clubhouse. For example, members visiting the Clubhouse more frequently (daily vs. monthly) and staying longer (3 hours or more) scored higher on measures of social competence and problem-solving competence than those participating less. The Youth Impact Survey results from nearly 4,000 members showed that among members who visited every day, 60% scored average or above on measures of social competence (social goals, initiation, and conflict management), compared to 49% of members who came monthly. Among members who stayed longer than 3 hours, 61% scored average or above, compared to only 49% of members who attended for less than an hour.

The surveys also showed that members who visited the Clubhouse more frequently and stayed longer scored higher on measures of problem-solving competence (problem-solving confidence and general problem solving). This research found that 60% of members who visited every day scored average or above compared with 52% of members who went monthly. Likewise, 63% of members who stayed for longer than 3 hours scored average or above, compared with 47% who stayed less than an hour.

These connections between Clubhouse participation and the development of twenty-first-century skills are reinforced by comments from Clubhouse participants themselves. Reflecting the emphasis in the Clubhouse on collaboration and peer mentoring, two Clubhouse members commented:

> I have helped the younger Clubhouse members with programs they didn't understand. Like Photoshop, Flash, and the rest with my anime drawings. I use my own illustrations in the Clubhouse and the young[er] members have seen my drawings and asked me would I teach them how to draw some anime pictures.

> If a member of the Clubhouse would ask me for help, I would stop what I am doing and help them with that they need. I watched a Clubhouse member on the 3-D Game Maker and was interested in it. I asked him

FIGURE 10.3. Social competence, by visit length and frequency

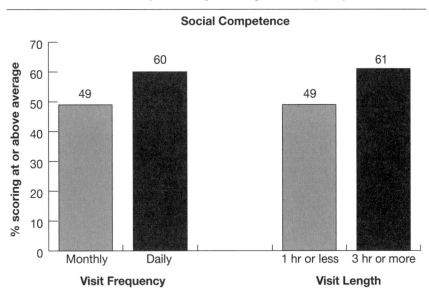

FIGURE 10.4. Problem-solving competence, by visit length and frequency

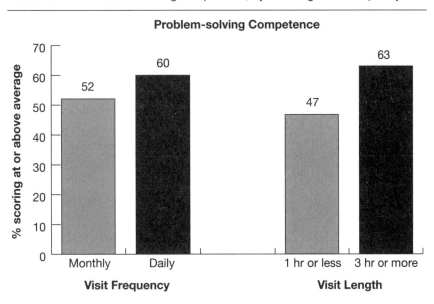

Note: Youth Impact Survey data (2005–07) from 3,732 Clubhouse member responses from 92 Clubhouses.

would he show me how it worked. This made him feel happy that I asked him to help me.

SRI's research points to a number of features of the Clubhouse environment that support the development of twenty-first-century skills:.

- Broad and integrated themes around which learning is built: Members develop their own themes and lines of interest around which to build projects for themselves.
- Problem identification and solution: Problems are authentic as part of the projects that youth undertake; if something isn't working, members need to figure out what the problem is and how to solve it.
- Relevance: The latitude given to members in choosing their activities and role models within the Clubhouse allows them to make what they do relevant to their life goals and interests.
- Active exploration: Clubhouse members have the opportunity for hands-on, problem-oriented, and open-ended "learning by doing."
- Choice and autonomy: Clubhouse activities are chosen by members.
- Cycle of creation: Members are engaged in multistage extended projects, encouraging revision.
- Collaboration and communication: Collaboration is built into the Clubhouse model, across activities.
- Authentic feedback: Self-assessment and reflection, peer criticism, and authentic opportunities for feedback on members' projects, often in the form of "showcases" that invite constructive input from peers and colleagues.
- Instructor as facilitator and mentor: The Clubhouse model minimizes didacticism and builds relationships of trust between the coordinator and members.

The second broad set of findings with respect to Clubhouse outcomes has to do with life pathways and members' capacities to follow these pathways to success. Recent research shows that young people who lack the ability to visualize the next steps in their lives are most likely to lose interest in education and eventually drop out of school. The Clubhouse provides an important means for young people to see the relevance to their lives of the skills they are developing and using every day, as well as for them to understand their own potential as productive, successful citizens of tomorrow.

In fact, the Clubhouse youth impact survey shows a strong correlation between Clubhouse participation and young people's sense of their own futures. For a list of the survey questions, see the series of reports titled Youth Impact Survey Results available on the Computer Clubhouse Network Web site (http://www.computerclubhouse.org/reports.htm). Based again on survey responses from nearly 4,000 youth from 2005 to 2007, SRI's quantitative assessment of Clubhouse outcomes showed strong effects for members' sense of their own futures (Figure 10.5). A sense of the future was significantly stronger for members who stay longer

FIGURE 10.5. Sense of future, by visit length and frequency

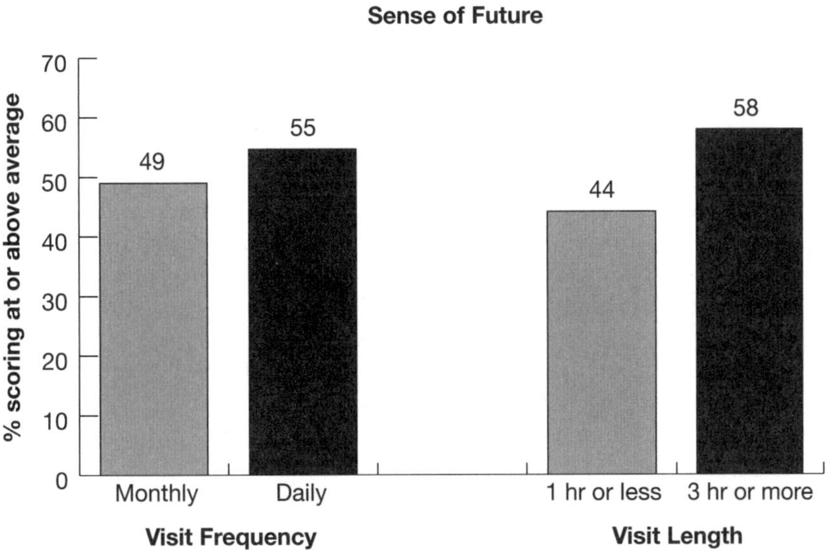

Note: Youth Impact Survey data (2005–07) from 3,732 Clubhouse member responses from 92 Clubhouses.

(3 or more hours), with 58% scoring at or above average compared to only 44% of participants whose visits are shorter (less than one hour). Sense of the future was also significantly stronger for members who visit more often (55% versus 49%).

School engagement and academic self-perception are also positively correlated with Clubhouse participation, as are young people's aspirations for the future. Against a backdrop of low college participation rates for underserved socioeconomic groups, SRI's research between 2005 and 2007 found that 76% of youth who visit Clubhouses on a daily basis plan to continue their education, as opposed to 66% of youth who visit only monthly. Similarly, 75% of members who stay longer than 3 hours aspire to higher education, compared to 66% of youth who make shorter visits.

But ask any Clubhouse coordinator about the ways in which the Clubhouse has supported their youth in making positive choices about the future and finding pathways to success, and they will illustrate the case not with survey results and quantitative data but with stories about individual youth facing often enormous challenges and succeeding, thanks to the support and inspiration they found in the Clubhouse. In fact, the young people will tell you these stories themselves:

> I owe a lot to the Intel Computer Clubhouse. In the 2 years I have been there, I learned a lot, not just about computers but myself. As a result of the positive reinforcement, I stayed in school where before I did not care. The Intel Computer Clubhouse was my U-turn. Since then I have passed all my classes and made [up] for lost ground.

Right now I'm working on anything that applies sociology and technology skills. But I don't want to stay in a cubicle. I'm interested in changing society, and have interests in urban planning, media, and art . . . lots of different things!

Another youth—now an alumnus in graduate school studying computer science—reports:

I realized I could mope around and do nothing, and I saw other people doing that. But that's not what I wanted to do. I wanted to keep coming here and developing my skills, and decided I was just going to keep coming to the Clubhouse.

The third broad area of outcomes is the commitment to community and service fostered by the Clubhouse culture. From the founding days of the Clubhouse, an underlying theme has been the responsibility that young people have to each other and to the Clubhouse community as "members." Many Clubhouse youth—and staff, for that matter—describe the Clubhouse as a second home or second family to them. In fact, on September 11, 2001, staff at the Flagship Clubhouse at the Museum of Science in Boston decided to stay open throughout the day, and were amazed to see streams of Clubhouse members wander in, one after the other, for comfort and support, just to be in each other's company. Clubhouse alumni often visit the Clubhouse on weekends or when they are home from college. Clubhouse anniversary parties are flooded with alumni who are there to celebrate their Clubhouse and its longtime success. Not surprisingly, SRI's Youth Impact Survey analysis between 2005 and 2007 showed that Clubhouse members' sense of belonging (general sense of belonging, relationship with adults) is higher for youth who participate more deeply (see Figure 10.6). Fifty-four percent of members who participated in Clubhouse activities daily scored above average on an item that measured sense of belonging compared with only 40% of members who visited only monthly (Figure 10.7). Likewise, 56% of members who visited for an extended period of time (3 or more hours) reported an above average sense of belonging compared with only 41% of participants whose visits were short.

But the notion of the Clubhouse as a community to which each member holds shared responsibility runs deep in the Clubhouse culture. Additionally, many Clubhouse youth look beyond the four walls of their Clubhouse and turn their sights outward to address issues in their own neighborhoods. Members at one Clubhouse whose town was holding local elections identified several issues important to young people in the community (e.g., relations between youth and the police, lack of green spaces for young people to play sports), and invited political candidates and the public to an evening discussion forum at the Clubhouse. The youth made minidocumentaries illustrating their concerns about each issue, and engaged the candidates in a discussion about what they would do to address them, if elected. In one evening, Clubhouse members discovered not only that they had a voice but that—through the resources of the Clubhouse and their own skills at utilizing those resources—they had a means for their voice to be heard.

FIGURE 10.6. Sense of belonging, by visit length and frequency

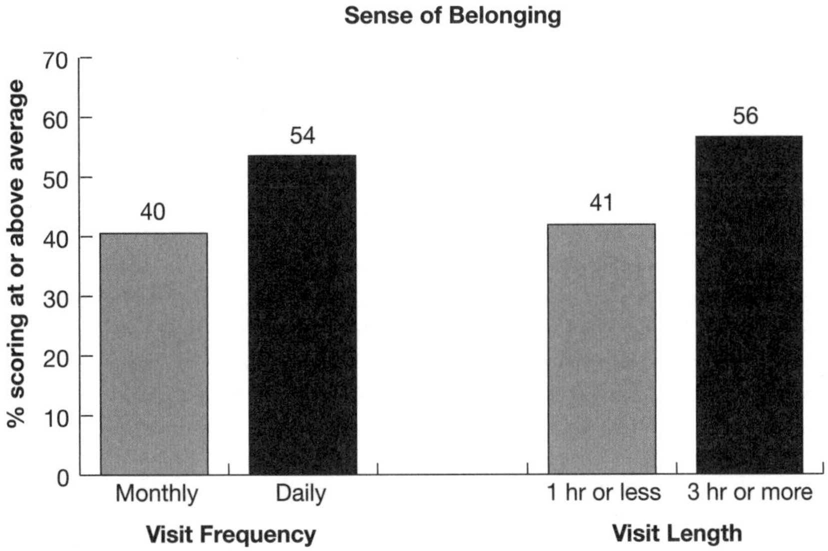

Sense of Belonging

Note: Youth Impact Survey data (2005–07) from 3,732 Clubhouse member responses from 92 Clubhouses.

Through the participation and engagement of the public, they also saw how their own action provided an important contribution to the community as a whole.

As the Clubhouse Network has grown to over 100 Clubhouses in more than 20 different countries, Clubhouse members have increasingly embraced their responsibility to the broader Network. Through the Clubhouse Village, Clubhouse members have the means to share what they know with others around the world, and to collaborate in ways that take them far beyond their local neighborhoods and communities.

FUTURE DIRECTIONS

In a world of unlimited resources, future research to explore the impact of the Clubhouse on young people's lives would entail tracking specific Clubhouse members from one year to the next, investigating how their attitudes and behaviors change over time, identifying the impact of the Clubhouse versus other influences, and linking outcomes with specific features of the Clubhouse model. But in the absence of unlimited resources, the Clubhouse Network plans to continue its current efforts to understand and document Clubhouse impact on youth, both quantitatively and qualitatively. As the number of Clubhouse alumni grows with time, we are identifying ways to better stay in touch, learn about their lives and how the Clubhouse has influenced their choices and life directions, and document those life stories.

It is our hope and expectation that these efforts will help to promote the development of additional Clubhouses in communities of need, as well as help to introduce Clubhouse ideas and practices to community technology centers and other educational institutions interested in adopting specific aspects of the Clubhouse learning model.

At the occasion of the opening of the 100th Computer Clubhouse in 2005, I was often asked, What is next, after 100? Although we reached an important milestone in establishing 100 Clubhouses, our work isn't done. As long as organizations reach out with the commitment and capacity to serve youth through the Computer Clubhouse program, the Intel Computer Clubhouse Network is dedicated to continuing to introduce the Clubhouse to new young people and new communities. In addition, we will continue to support the ongoing efforts of Clubhouses around the Network, by providing professional development and materials for Clubhouse staff, offering opportunities for Clubhouse youth leaders such as the Teen Summit and college scholarships, and by serving as a catalyst for Clubhouses around the network to share best practices, ideas, successes, and resources with each other.

The success of the Intel Computer Clubhouse Network is due to the many community-based organizations and staff that have embraced the mission of the Computer Clubhouse, as well as the sponsors that have supported their efforts. And of course it is due to the thousands of youth who have participated in Clubhouses over the years "voting with their feet" to spend their time in positive, productive, empowering ways. In short, our work is not yet done, nor will it be until the Digital Divide that the Clubhouse attempts to address—and the social, economic, and educational divides that equally serve as sorrowful motivators for our work—have finally been closed.

NOTES

Most of the evaluation reports can be found at the Intel Computer Clubhouse Network Web site, including the "Computer Clubhouse Network Assessment and Planning Report Summary, July–December 2007" (http://www.computerclubhouse.org/reports.htm) and reports from the "Computer Clubhouse Alumni: Where Are They Now?" (http://www.computerclubhouse.org/spotlight/alumni.htm).

Over the past 10 years two independent research and evaluation firms, Education Development Center's Center for Children and Technology, based in New York, and SRI International's Center for Technology in Learning, based in Menlo Park, California have been conducting assessments and in-depth participation analyses commissioned by the Museum of Science in Boston with funding from the Intel Foundation. The findings presented in this chapter have been drawn from these reports, as well as Clubhouse self-assessment and planning reports.

Chapter 11

Hear Our Voices: Girls Developing Technology Fluency

Brenda Abanavas and Robbin Chapman

On any given Monday, the Girls' Day at the Flagship Clubhouse is a hive of activity and creative energy. Music and laughter, two girls huddled over some project, excited chattering of girls gathered at a worktable. Girls are working on an array of projects, from 3-D graphics design to making music beats to programming storybook animations. Around a green table in the center of the room, a group of girls are exchanging project ideas. Across from them, two girls giggle as they leaf through an art book for inspiration. Most noticeable is the ease with which the girls are using the computer technology, commanding the physical space, and engaging with each other. Girls' voices seem to emanate from every nook and cranny of the room.

While the Clubhouse has provided thousands of youth with opportunities to learn by engaging in self-motivated projects, Girls' Day has not always been part of the Computer Clubhouse. In fact, it often appeared that girls were not benefiting from access to the resources in the same way that boys were. Girls were not working on increasingly complex design projects (Gallagher, Michalchik, & Emery, 2006). Instead, they were pursuing activities like surfing the Web or e-mailing. In some cases, girls were relegated to playing an ornamental role of just sitting and watching boys work. Girls were not having success competing for Clubhouse equipment and resources with their male counterparts.

Social pressures embedded in the larger society have impacted how boys and girls interact in the Clubhouse. They have told girls that they are not the technology users or creators and that technology is for boys. As a result, girls viewed technology as male and off-limits (Corbett & St. Rose, 2008; Chapman, 2001). These messages often led to girls foregoing engagement with technology as fully as boys. In the Clubhouse this translated as girls either not working on projects or not staying engaged when confronted with more challenging project activities.

This chapter presents the lessons learned from a program called Hear Our Voices (HOV), which was designed to support girls becoming technology savvy within the Computer Clubhouse. HOV was implemented at 20 Clubhouses in the United States over a 3-year period. Some Clubhouses had offered girls' programming earlier on, pursuant to local needs. The HOV program recognized the need for focused girls' programming and evaluation of program impact across the Intel Clubhouse Network. We will look at how the first program under the HOV grant was implemented at the Flagship Clubhouse in Boston. Then we will present some lessons learned from various HOV sites about growing these kinds of programs. Finally, we will summarize some results of an evaluation of the program and discuss the implications of programs like HOV for all young learners.

THE GIRLS' DAY PROGRAM: HEAR OUR VOICES

HOV was designed to connect girls more deeply to technology by providing them access to female role models, other girls with interests in technology, and a supportive, accessible learning environment. A program goal was to improve girls' viewpoint about technology and working with technology. As the name suggests, HOV strives to make girls' voices heard, both literally and through their projects. HOV has the following guiding principles:

- Inspire and excite girls and young women to become self-motivated, confident learners through the use of technology by engaging them in hands-on, participatory experiences that make learning fun
- Empower girls and young women to become productive contributors to their communities and recognize they can excel in a technological career world
- Expose girls to influential women, emphasizing positive character and leadership traits
- Provide educators and community leaders a model for using computer technology for experimentation, design, self-expression, creativity, and collaboration for girls and young women

With funding from the National Science Foundation (NSF) in 2003, HOV was launched at 10 Clubhouses within its first year. In the second year, another 10 additional HOV programs were established. A unique characteristic of HOV is the attention given to leveraging the particular resources of each Clubhouse's host organization. Program developers recognized the host organization would need to make adjustments to provide girls with appropriate HOV spaces, staffing, resource allocation, and strategies for postgrant girls' programming sustainability. To ensure these needs were address, the HOV grant required host organizations to meet the following program requirements:

- Hire a dedicated HOV coordinator for a minimum of 10 hours per week
- Introduce the HOV coordinator to her role and responsibilities through attendance at the Intel Computer Clubhouse Network (ICCN) network-run orientation

- Participate in monthly teleconferences with other HOV coordinators and the HOV program manager
- Recruit, train, and supervise mentors to work with girls and young women
- Recruit girls from underserved communities
- Develop a plan for fund raising to sustain the program after the initial NSF funding period
- Adapt an appropriate physical space for program operation
- Solicit input from the HOV Advisory Board

The grant covered costs such as a stipend to supplement coordinator salary, mentor development, Career-to-College (C2C) field trips, and guest speaker activities relevant to girls' interests and needs. HOV coordinators attended orientation on program implementation and were given program support and technical assistance from the Computer Clubhouse Network staff.

KEY PROGRAM FEATURES: REFLECTIVE MENTOR MODEL

A more in-depth examination of the operational processes revealed that when Clubhouse staff served as HOV coordinators, turnover was reduced and transfer of learning increased. But we also found that mentor retention was a major challenge. Sites that were able to retain their mentors saw increased program effectiveness. When we compared sites that served as "best models" for achieving successful programming goals to sites that saw more modest results, we found that partnering with local universities and professional women's organizations resulted in better and easier adherence to program specifications. Program staff who actively partnered with these local resources found that these collaborations aided in mentor recruitment and retention. Clubhouse-to-College/Clubhouse-to-Careers (C2C) activities included in the suite of HOV program activities also supported better outcomes.

But by far the most important success factor was the addition of enhancements to the Clubhouse mentor training and adoption of a pedagogy that adapted to the changing needs of a diverse pool of learners. The mentor model is called the *reflective mentor model* (Chapman, 2006) and the pedagogy is called *reflective pedagogy* (Chapman, 2007). The reflective mentor model utilizes the reflection-in-action and reflection-on-action activities described in Schön's (1983, 1987) reflective practitioner framework (Figure 11.1). Reflection-in-action occurs while a mentor is working with a learner, with the mentor dividing her attention between working with the learner and reflecting on what is and isn't working in the moment. This process allows the mentor to think on her feet in order to stay one step ahead of the learner's needs. Reflection-on-action occurs when the cohort of mentors is together after learners have left for the day. Mentors discuss strategies that did or did not lead to the achievement of learning objectives. Team reflection is a mechanism for mentors to leverage past lessons learned to inform their future mentoring.

FIGURE 11.1. Reflective mentor model

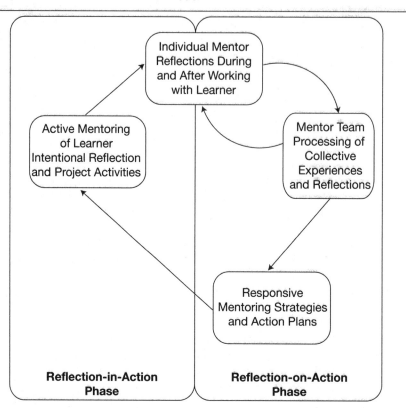

Individual Mentor Reflections During and After Working with Learner

Active Mentoring of Learner Intentional Reflection and Project Activities

Mentor Team Processing of Collective Experiences and Reflections

Responsive Mentoring Strategies and Action Plans

Reflection-in-Action Phase

Reflection-on-Action Phase

Reflective Mentoring

Mentors were a critical element of the HOV success. Program guidelines required mentors to receive comprehensive training about the Clubhouse learning model and information on girls' development, both learning and leadership. They required mentors to focus on moving girls' learning to the next level as a "normal part" of mentoring. Mentors were challenged to do this "in the moment" while working with a girl and through later consultation with other mentors. These group consultations took place after Clubhouse hours when the group got together to evaluate how girls fared at the clubhouse that day. Mentors shared best practices, frustrations, and challenges in guiding girls toward increasingly complex design activities. The mentor team then converged on strategies to deploy on the next girls' day. For example, a strategy for better connecting girls with similar project interests required the mentors to know all the girls better. They implemented this strategy by having each mentor connect with two girls that they had not met before. Over time mentors gained a handle on each girl's interest and were able to broker connections and collaborations between those girls. The mentors later used what they had learned to encourage girls to troubleshoot each other's projects. The goal was to be supportive while also challenging girls to engage in increasingly complex project and design activities. These regular reflection sessions played an important role in mentor retention. Sessions were viewed as professional development opportunities. Mentors commented that group reflection helped them do a better job in later encounters with the girls:

> I've learned so much listening to how we deal with the issues that come up during the day. I certainly don't think I can figure out all the right answers by myself. Besides, I think we're doing a better job when we all know what the other is doing and we all go in with the same overall goal in mind.

> When it came to my own learning with the other mentors, I got a lot from hearing their hands-on ideas and problem solving. It was nice getting to know them better too; it's so hard while the members are here to do that, unless you just ignore the members but that's not why I'm here.

> I'm here to learn how to be a better mentor. I'm not going to stay late every week if I'm not going to get something out of it. I see this team as our time to practice for next Monday. We're more professional that way. All this reviewing and planning we do. I think that says we're serious about learning in the Clubhouse. I feel like I really know what I'm supposed to be here for and I like that.

Reflective mentors learned by constructing and reconstructing their approach to mentoring. Rather than creating a definitive best practice, a set of evolving best practices responsive to the needs of learners and the learning environment was being invented and reinvented. Mentoring became a cycle of working with youth, garnering new experiences, reflecting on those experiences, both individually and as a team, and converging on corrective strategies.

Reflective Pedagogy

Reflective pedagogy was a mechanism mentors used to build important connections between girls and others. The quality of these connections seemed to impact how well the girls acclimated to being in the Clubhouse, how well they bonded with other girls, and how willing they were to take risks and tackle design challenges. The types of connections developed included:

- Girl-to-girl
- Mentor-to-girl
- Project-to-girl
- Clubhouse-to-girl

Each connection type characterizes important ways in which girls' interactions help with their identity development and growth as learners and leaders.

These connections have all proved important to each girl's success in HOV. Figure 11.2 details aspects of each type of connection.

HOV mentors often considered how these various connections could be created and strengthened. They recognized that different girls have different needs at different times, and being able to identify what type of "disconnects" were occurring helped mentors think about how to help learners get back on track.

LEARNING ACROSS THE HOV NETWORK

Many lessons from across the HOV network were shared through monthly coordinator meetings and postings to the HOV section of the Clubhouse Village (see Chapter 2). The Clubhouse Village was a valuable tool for coordinating the efforts and learning of HOV coordinators and mentors. Online resources included a dedicated HOV Web site, relevant information, and shared stories of best practices and programming ideas. HOV coordinators used the Village to develop strategies for sustaining the program. One discussion thread was about working with their respective host organizations to better promote the HOV program. HOV mentors used the Village to share best practices. For the girls, the Village provided a mechanism for showcasing their projects. Over the course of the program, the quantity of girls' projects that were posted on the Village increased significantly.

LESSONS LEARNED

A formula for growing a program that builds connections between girls and technology is not simple or straightforward. However, the requisite building blocks to an HOV-like program began to emerge as the various HOV sites began to share their lessons learned. These building blocks addressed specific aspects of program development, mentor development, and girls' development.

Program Development

- Ensure that girls' interests—whatever they may be in the local setting—should be the core of any project development and program activities.
- Encourage use of current Clubhouse staff as HOV staff. This reduces instances of turnover and increases transfer of learning from girls-only to regular days.
- Collaborate with local agencies that serve girls' needs. These connections can aid in recruiting girls, recruiting mentors, and providing a variety of additional resources.
- Partner with mentors from other days, especially male mentors. This will facilitate moving girls back into other days at the Clubhouse.

FIGURE 11.2. Connections that impact the quality of girls' engagement with technology

Type of Connection	Features of Connection
Girl-to-girl:	Girls like to work together to design their projects. HOV mentors worked to strengthen relationships between the girls within the program. Attention was given to team-building activities and cooperative projects. Mentors also monitored group dynamics. If there were problems between girls, mentors used these instances as learning opportunities for constructive problem resolution.
Mentor-to-girl:	Mentors got to know each girl, her interests, and her current level of proficiency with technology. Girls were encouraged to "sample" the design tools at the Clubhouse. This allowed girls to experience new technologies and expand their repertoire of design ideas for incorporation into their projects. Girls were encouraged to practice taking risks rather than always doing the comfortable thing. This taught girls to experience discomfort and still move ahead with their projects.
Project-to-girl:	Starting out with appropriate pedagogies is a powerful tool for engaging girls with their projects. The rule of thumb is, "start where the girls are." When girls first arrived at the Clubhouse, mentors helped them gain confidence by first finding out what their interests are and guiding them to projects centered on those interests. Mentors also suggested more collaborative and more socially meaningful projects, which seemed to capture the girls' attention. Mentors discovered that learning about how a particular technology worked needed to be coupled with the affective values that make the project meaningful for the girls. Clubhouse-to-College/Clubhouse-to-Careers activities (field trips, workshops, guest speakers, etc.) helped girls make important connections between their developing technology and design skills and the world of work and school. Making these connections was critical to retaining girls in the program.
Clubhouse-to-girl:	It was always intended for HOV to move girls from solely attending girls' day toward attending on other clubhouse days as well. There was also the intention to move boys toward engaging in more girls' day type of experiences. Girls' day was not exclusionary. Boys are not the enemy or the competition. This idea was made clear and discussed among girls' day members and mentors. There have been some efforts to bring boys into the girls' day space, with very specific goals in mind. Boys have attended as mentors or to conduct workshops. They went through a rigorous interview process to ascertain their motivations for working with the girls. They received orientation on girls' day culture and were reminded that they were visitors to the girls' day program. The Flagship Computer Clubhouse, in Boston, has experimented with bringing older clubhouse boys in as mentors. In some HOV programs, there was initial concern on the coordinator's part that girls would not welcome the boys. In a series of discussions, girls worked out their expectations were for that mentor. The experiment was successful. Girls worked well with male mentors. Also, when mentors attended the clubhouse on other days, they helped bring a new perspective on relationships between female and male clubhouse members. Boys gained newly found respect and appreciation for the girls. Another connection between the clubhouse and girls was seen as girls and their work became more visible, both inside and outside their local clubhouses. Girls exhibited projects at art shows, exhibitions, on community television, and in museum installations. At monthly clubhouse showcases, they made presentations of their completed projects and projects in progress. This gave girls a chance to be recognized by their peers.

Mentor Development

- Ensure that mentor training includes building a knowledge base about girls' development.
- Provide adequate numbers of mentors so that girls have ample coverage. Adequate mentor coverage impacts girls' willingness to push through challenges with technology.
- Develop a skilled mentor pool by maintaining a consistent training regime. Any training should be in the context with the activities occurring in the Clubhouse. Such professional mentor development is a valuable retention tool and makes mentors more effective with the girls.

Girls' Development

- Identify activities that aid in girls' leadership development and build confidence. For example, train girls to become peer mentors as they become more savvy users.
- Ensure that girls and their projects are a presence in the Clubhouse. Have girls post their work, online and in the physical space. Encourage them to showcase their projects.
- Introduce the girls to women in education and industry and connect their Clubhouse project experiences to future career opportunities. That helps girls make connections between their "real lives" and opportunities open to them via their clubhouse learning.
- Provide snacks for the girls. Eating together was part of the social bonding process. That gave girls a chance to connect without technology as the conduit. Peer bonding was particularly effective in building enthusiasm for tackling more challenging projects. Also, it helped foster an environment that served to deepen learning relationships and promote project collaboration.
- Initiate girls to technology by "starting where the girls are" in respect to ability, interests, and types of projects.
- Provide opportunities for the girls to strengthen their relationships with their peers. Girls place a lot of importance on peer relationships.

These lessons about the program, mentors, and girls' development emerged as HOV sites learned how to best help girls enjoy richer interactions with their projects and each other. The following excerpts from HOV quarterly reports describe some of the types of projects and initiatives girls were becoming involved in.

We've made personalized calendars using Microsoft Publisher and bound them for the girls to take home as gifts. Girls are creating PowerPoint portfolios of their artwork, movies, original music, and career plans. Several members have made movies using stop animation. Two girls made music videos using Adobe Premier and Karaoke Dream software.

March was the month for Flash [multimedia software] and we had several girls become quick masters, creating animations over 100 frames long in their first sitting. The nights when we worked with Flash really emphasized how great our girl-to-mentor ratio is because the girls never had to wait long for help and so didn't get the chance to get frustrated and give up! . . . One particular animation was very clever: a caterpillar whose face parts all moved individually to create some very clever expressions!

During this reporting period the girls worked on several projects using the Corel software. The girls have used Rave [animation software], Paint [graphics software], and Bryce [3-D landscape design software] to complete different projects. They used Rave to do Christmas animations and Bryce to create background scenes.

Across the HOV sites, girls were engaged in increasingly complex projects relevant to their interest and therefore worth struggling through any design challenges that came up. Over time, as girls posted projects on Clubhouse walls and on the Village intranet, the success of the program did not go unnoticed by the boys. Some approached the girls to inquire about their projects. At several sites the boys began requesting similar programs for themselves.

EVALUATION APPROACH

Researchers from the Wellesley Centers for Women at Wellesley College (Erkut & Marx, 2005) evaluated 14 of the 20 HOV Clubhouse sites. The purpose of the evaluation was to document HOV operations over time and tease out those elements that contributed to program success. The evaluation focused on the overall impact of the HOV program on girls' experiences and learning with technology and looked at the changes in girls' attitudes toward technology and how important girls rated those technologies as having a positive impact on their lives. Data was collected from coordinator quarterly reports, attendance reports, site visits, and surveys that measured program impact on girls. Survey participants included 151 girls from 14 HOV sites. Surveys were administered at Time 1 (September and October 2004) and Time 2 (April and May 2005). Racial/ethnic distributions across all the sites were Black/African American (38%), Latina/Chicana (31%), Multiethnic (16%), and Caucasian/White (11%). The average age was 11.37 years.

THE EFFECT OF HOV ON GIRLS

The evaluation indicated that HOV girls-only interventions met program goals in various ways. Girls were attempting more challenging and complex projects. The percentage of girls who were engaging in more complex learning activities increased from 10% to 20% during a 7-month period. Also, girls indicated that their attendance in the girls-day program gave them increased opportunity to work on more complex projects. Girls developed awareness of the relevance of computers to their lives and to their future aspirations. Again, their relationships with mentors were a powerful predictor of this increased awareness. Participation in the program also increased girls' interest in attending the coed days at the Clubhouse. Their return to the coed Clubhouse environment stemmed from increased self-confidence and increased opportunities to showcase their work. These and other changes noted over the course of the HOV study and evaluation speak directly to obstacles that have limited girls' engagement with computer technology.

HOV participants have come away with new insights about themselves and their relationship with technology:

> [My HOV participation] has changed the way I think about the world through technology. It has made me understand, to create and explore new challenges.

> I found out I could do things on a computer that look hard, but are really easier than I thought.

> [My HOV participation] shows me I can do things that I have never done, before such as make movies. I also build robots.

A small number of girls indicated that the HOV program was incidental to the completion of their projects. These girls expressed that they didn't benefit specifically from HOV because they didn't need a girls-only environment to get their Clubhouse projects done.

> I would come if there are no girls because I like to learn things and not play with my friends that are girls.

> Yes, [I would come] because I'd still be with friends and staff that are there.

Different aspects of the HOV program were salient for different girls. Half of the girls reported that developing relationships with their peers and increased self-knowledge were changes they perceived in themselves while participating in HOV. The evaluations revealed that girls did want to try more complex and interesting projects. It also revealed that a positive, responsive learning environment and programs are critical to making meaningful connections between girls and computer technologies.

CONCLUSIONS

HOV is not the usual "add girls and stir" model. Program developers did not attempt to "adjust" the way girls think and learn to fit better prevailing project styles and ways of working at the Clubhouse. They also did not design a program that reflected a monolithic view of "girl learning." Although targeted at developing girls' fluency with technology, the program's foundation was grounded in supporting multiple ways of learning across a diverse group of learners. For this reason, HOV has broad educational value. We could imagine how HOV could provide similar benefits to boys. HOV's strength is the program's capacity to adapt to differing motivations for learner engagement. It was important to attend to, recognize, and respond to those multiple motivations for engaging Clubhouse girls. At the Flagship Clubhouse particular attention was given to developing mentor skills and pedagogies that were responsive to girls' learning needs, both individual and as a group.

What we learned in the process is that girls are interested in technology. The challenge is how to interweave technology into more aspects of their lives. This richer engagement can impact the social, cultural, and financial outcomes of these future women. The lessons of HOV inform us how to better support girls' learning with and making meaningful connections to technology. These lessons reach beyond girls' day and contribute to our understanding of how learning environments like the Clubhouse can successfully support diverse ways of knowing and learning.

Chapter 12

From Photoshop to Programming

Yasmin Kafai, Kylie Peppler, Grace Chiu, John Maloney, Natalie Rusk, and Mitchel Resnick

Walk into any Computer Clubhouse and you are likely to see members creating and manipulating graphics, animations, videos, music, and often integrating multiple media. The professional image-processing tool, Adobe Photoshop, is particularly popular. Indeed, a "Photoshop culture" has emerged at many Clubhouses, with youth proudly displaying their visual creations on bulletin boards in the Clubhouse and in the Village, sharing Photoshop techniques and ideas with one another, and helping Clubhouse newcomers get started with the software. Clubhouse members, like many youth today, are familiar with a wide range of design tools they can use on computers for creative production; programming tools, however, are most often not considered part of this portfolio (Margolis, 2008).

As a case in point, we report on our observations in the Youth Opportunities Unlimited Inc. Computer Clubhouse that was opened in 2001 and thus is perhaps more typical of other Clubhouses in the network than the Flagship, with its longstanding history. Two full-time coordinators run the day-to-day operations and facilitate activities at the Clubhouse with the help of several mentors (see Chapter 8). From observations in 2003–2004, we knew that programming activities did not occur. Although Microworlds software, a visual Logo computer programming software, was available as part of a broad suite of software, neither adult coordinators nor members used it. While the most popular software titles enabled multiple media integration and manipulation, programming was considered a "stand alone" task and was therefore perceived as incompatible and irrelevant to existing popular design activities. How programming became part of this one Clubhouse's portfolio of design activities and what members learned and how they thought about programming will be the focus of this chapter.

THE DESIGN OF A NEW PROGRAMMING TOOL—SCRATCH

Through prior observations at the Clubhouses, we found that youth have an interest in video games, music videos, cartoon animations, and interactive, design-based art, all of which are a natural springboard into creating and programming.

Thus we started with addressing the overly narrow notion of programming by focusing on the cultural artifacts that it could produce. This led us to recognize the benefits of programming as creative media production, which included a broader range of digital artifacts, ranging from video games to "media mixes" of images, video, and texts. With that in mind, we set out to create a media-rich programming environment, called Scratch (see Chapter 4), which would provide youth with the ability to import and manipulate various media files that could be integrated with existing creative software. Arguably a full-fledged programming language, Scratch vastly differs from other novice-friendly visual programming environments in that it utilizes a user-friendly building block command structure, eliminating the risk of syntax errors. More information about the design of Scratch can be found in Resnick et al. (2003) and Maloney et al. (2004).

Our observations revealed that several pathways into the programming culture evolved over time at the Clubhouse. One of the coordinators introduced Scratch in late 2004. Although Scratch was loaded on several of the computers at this time, fewer than 10 members took advantage and created anything using the new software. Beginning in 2005 a steady stream of undergraduate mentors joined the Clubhouse and the first explosion of Scratch activity was seen starting in early January 2005. Youth were encouraging one another to try out the program, and mentors worked with youth to create their first Scratch projects. Commonly, mentors would engage youth who had never worked in Scratch before by suggesting that they import some of the pictures that they had stored in their folders on the Clubhouse server (see Chapter 8). At this point in time the server featured a predominance of graphics-only projects that lacked any computer programming, which was due in part to the high volume of youth opening the program without any official orientation. Printouts of projects quickly began to cover the walls, and Scratch became the leading design activity within a few months of its introduction.

In the beginning of 2006 there was an even greater interest in Scratch and some new things began happening within the Clubhouse culture. Scratch was used among the youth as a measure of membership in the local culture: New members wanting to establish clear membership in the community had to first create at least one Scratch project and store it for others to play on the central server. For the first time, more expert youth were seen mentoring other youth in Scratch. Scratch experts had a high-status position within the local culture, with some youth emerging as general experts, whom mentors, coordinators, and other youth consulted for help with Scratch, and other youth specializing in certain genres or tricks within Scratch. In addition, groups of youth had begun working collaboratively together to create projects with a group name, such as DGMM, for the Dang Good Money Makers. Youth also began to work independently of mentoring support, reflective of the high volume of projects beginning in June 2006, on complex projects and problems that they encountered in Scratch.

THE CLUBHOUSE DESIGN CULTURE

To further understand the impact of introducing new design software into the Clubhouse environment, we examined in 213 field notes the design focus of various activities distinguishing between design, games, Web, homework, and social activities. A subset consisting of 64 field notes was coded by four graduate students and revealed a reliability of 85–92%. Design activities involved the use of programming, 3-D animation, and graphic software such as Kai's SuperGoo, Bryce5, Photoshop, KidPix, game design programs such as RPG Maker, and music production software. Game activities included games on the computer, such as Roller Coaster (Tycoon), School Tycoon, video and online games, such as Whyville.net, as well as board and card games, foosball, and air hockey. Web activities involved Web surfing with a Clubhouse member, while homework involved mentors helping youth with their homework. We also created a "Personal" category to include all social activities and interactions between the mentor and Clubhouse youth that establish and build upon the interpersonal relationship outside of the context of the other activities. We interpret these findings as being a proxy for Clubhouse activities, of which we would otherwise have no indication.

One general outcome is that programming activities increased as Scratch became embedded in the popular suite of design tools that Clubhouse members utilized on a daily basis (Kafai, Peppler, & Chiu, 2007). Initially, design activities comprised about 70% of all Clubhouse member activities followed by homework (14%), Web surfing (8%), and games (8%). After Scratch was introduced, it comprised 25% of all activities while other design activities accounted for 18%, followed by an increased interest in games (30%) and personal activities (17%), while homework and web Surfing decreased (5% each).

The design portfolio illustrates how programming had become part of the Clubhouse activities. Over the course of 2 years we tracked Scratch development and collected all projects created by Clubhouse members. There were several reasons for this approach, but important to the purposes of this chapter is that it allowed us to peek at the computing culture when even mentors and researchers were not present. The number of new Scratch projects is also a good indication of general interest in computer programming over time. We observed that the majority of interest in Scratch occurs from January through August, and there was less interest in the fall months between September and December. This is probably due to several reasons, but can be somewhat explained by the presence of mentors from January through March. There was also a high volume of projects being created over the summer months (especially in June and July of 2006) in the absence of extensive mentoring support. We interpret this as an indication of the extended and prolonged impact that mentoring support can have on a programming culture beyond (or at least temporarily beyond) the weekly visits of the mentors.

LOCAL DESIGN CULTURES: THE LOW RIDA PROJECTS

The total number of Scratch projects paints a picture of an active computing culture, but what exactly are youth creating in Scratch? Because Scratch was designed to flexibly promote self-expression, youth appropriated the software in a number of ways. Over the course of 18 months, we collected 536 programming projects created by members of the Clubhouse, some designed alone and others with mentors

(Kafai, Peppler, Alavez, & Ruvalcaba, 2006). We found that 44% of these projects fell into the category of animations with and without user manipulation, followed by 23% of graphics-only projects, and 15% of game projects focusing on fighting, sports, and adventure; 14% of projects escaped a clear categorization because they did not provide enough detail. The quantitative changes in design and mentoring activities were accompanied by qualitative changes in Scratch program genres and Clubhouse members' conceptions of programming.

Some youth emerged who took on strong leadership roles. These leaders began to work with groups of 10–12 other youth to seemingly manufacture certain genres of projects; one example of this is the Low Rida movement that began in January 2006. Within urban youth cultures there is a lot of interest in customizing cars. Television shows, like MTV's *Pimp My Ride,* have popularized this trend within mainstream American culture. Previously in the Clubhouse, a popular activity was to manipulate digital pictures of expensive cars, inserting a picture of yourself next to "your" car. Made popular by a young biracial African American/ Latino youth named Dwight, a culture of Low Rida interactive art projects has emerged. In one of Dwight's first projects, "Low Low," the viewer controls the hydraulics on two cars using arrow and letter keys. According to Dwight, the essential parts to his "Low Rida" project are the cars, the urban background, the graffiti-like lettering, and the speakers (see Figure 12.1). It is important to note that the Low Rida movement emerged in the absence of mentoring support. The Clubhouse members conceptualized the idea and executed the projects almost entirely by themselves.

Several new Low Rida projects have emerged based on Dwight's earlier work, resulting in a widespread use of Scratch. In these projects, the creators have used Photoshop, Painter7, Image editors, and computer programming for creative production. By participating in the Low Rida movement, youth gain access to skills, empowering them to become designers of digital media. This is an important aspect of participation in an informal learning culture where contribution is valued. Projects like these eliminate barriers between high and low pop cultures by taking an urban youth culture theme and reinventing it using high-status knowledge, such as software design.

SCRATCH PROGRAMMING PERFORMANCES

In a further step, we used the archive of Scratch projects to analyze their content for programming scripts. While most programming assessments focus on various aspects of individual or team programmers' performances in coding and debugging a piece of software, here we decided to evaluate the performance of a community by examining the content of the archive for essential programming concepts. The goal of this analysis was to study the extent to which youth touched upon these concepts as well as to gauge if the community as a whole increased their knowledge of computer programming over time. Of the 536 projects, 111 of them contained no scripts at all. These "pre-scripting" projects illustrate the use of Scratch simply as a media manipulation and composition tool. Beginning Scratch

FIGURE 12.1. Screenshots of Dwight's "Low Rida" projects are in the upper and lower right corners. Other members of the clubhouse created the two other "Low Rida" Scratch projects. In the upper left, Dwight's brother customized his ride by painting it gold and drawing in gold hubcaps. In the lower left, an 8-year-old girl created her own version of the "Low Rida" project, inserting a portrait that she created of herself using Painter7 software.

users often spend time importing or drawing images and recording sounds before moving on to scripting.

Of the remaining 427 projects, all of them created scripts and 374 of them had scripts run in parallel. These are core ideas in programming that confront every Scratch programmer when they begin writing scripts. About half of the projects provided keyboard or mouse input for users of their programs. On the other end of the spectrum, variables, random numbers, or Boolean logic were only used in few projects; these are concepts that are not easily discovered on one's own. In fact, one Clubhouse member had a desperate need for the variables in his project. When Mitchel Resnick, on a visit to the Clubhouse, showed him how to use variables, he immediately saw how they could be used to solve his problems and thanked Mitchel repeatedly for the advice.

When we compared the distributions from the first year to the second year of our data collection, we found that four of the seven programming concepts (loops, Boolean logic, variables, and random numbers) demonstrated significant gains in the number of projects utilizing the targeted concepts. One of the remaining concepts (i.e., conditional statements) had marginal gains, and one concept (communication/synchronization) demonstrated a significant reduction in the number of projects utilizing this particular concept. For more detail see Maloney, Peppler, Kafai, Resnick, and Rusk (2008).

Given the popularity of games and animation, it is not surprising that projects showing user input were common. It was a pleasant surprise to find that the commands for synchronizing interactions between objects were also fairly heavily used; interobject communications is one of the most complex ideas in Scratch, but it answers a critical need when building more complex projects. On the other hand, Boolean operations, variables, and random numbers were less obvious objects. We also examined trends over time. In general, the number of projects produced in the second year doubled the number of projects produced during the same period the first year of the project. When we compared the percentage of projects containing the various programming concepts over time, we found that most of the concepts that we targeted for our analyses demonstrated significant gains during the second year.

PERCEPTIONS OF PROGRAMMING

What did the Clubhouse members in this study have to say about their Scratch programming experiences? We interviewed a large number of youth to better understand how they are making sense of and appropriating Scratch. Each interview lasted about 15–20 minutes and questions included the following: What is computer programming to you? Does Scratch remind you of anything that you do at school or at home? How does Scratch differ from other computer software programs? All of the interviews were transcribed in preparation for later analyses. Researchers coded for themes rather than individual statements because these were group interviews and participants often expressed agreements with statements voiced by others; thus we did not expect every participant to repeat impressions.

General conceptions of Scratch were overwhelmingly positive with Clubhouse members proclaiming that it's their "favoritest thing ever." According to youth, Scratch is extremely flexible and has no, or few, limitations. Having trouble defining what Scratch was exactly, most youth described it as "something that allows you to use your imagination" or as "a system that will allow you to do whatever you want." Most youth cited at least four to five different applications for which Scratch could be used, including making games, Low Ridas, comics, animations, music videos, short movies, and digital art. Although youth could recall a great deal about how to create projects in Scratch, citing specific commands and naming specific parts of the screen, most youth were unaware that creating in Scratch would be considered "computer programming." In fact, over half of the youth were unable to define what computer programming was.

If youth do not recognize that they are learning programming through Scratch, what do youth believe that they are gaining from their experience? Clubhouse members reported a wide range of connections to traditional subject areas such as math, reading, science, and foreign language learning, in addition to strong connections to the arts. The following excerpt is taken from an interview with Arnold, a 14-year-old African American boy with limited Scratch experience, as he recounts his personal connection to Scratch through his experience as an actor. Notably, he cites how drama could be extended and reinforced in certain ways through Scratch.

> *Arnold:* Well let me see . . . . Well Scratch it really brings out my potential and it actually brings out my acting experience.
> *Kylie:* How so?
> *Arnold:* Well when you take the microphone, you can create your own voice for your character. Like I love Arnold Schwarzenegger. Yeah it just really brings out your potential . . . . Thinking of what you're doing with acting you can take it out of your mind and say like "in this picture we want to like do action stunts like flips and stuff", and if you're at school you're like doing Romeo and Juliet. You can make it more funny [in Scratch] by putting in some dragons. You can make a dragon go up to a castle and say "I came to rescue you". . . . Then you put them all in their places [in Scratch] and then once we do "Action!" We all come in with our parts.

Although we don't intend for youth to become hacker types as a result of their experience in Scratch, the involvement in the design process has awakened new possible career opportunities for some of the youth, notably the teenage boys. As one member puts it, "It teaches how to play games and make games and it helps us figure out our future." This particular youth would now like to be a professional video game designer, to attend college at MIT, and perhaps someday design a program like Scratch. He revels in his conversations with the professional programmers of Scratch and thoughtfully comes up with suggestions for how to further revise Scratch. It's clear that experiences like the ones at this Computer Clubhouse can have a considerable impact on the outlook and career aspirations of young people. Clearly, this is an area worthy of further exploration if we intend for youth to enter the computer science pipeline through informal avenues of education.

Most youth didn't identify scripting in Scratch as a form of programming. In general, when youth were asked, "What is computer programming to you?" they responded: "Computer programming? I do not have a clue [what that is]!" At first we were concerned that youth didn't make the connection between Scratch and programming. But on reflection, not seeing Scratch as "programming" may have helped Scratch catch on, allowing youth to see Scratch as being in line with their identities as kids, as something "cool," and as a central part of the Clubhouse culture. After all, the point of engaging youth in computer programming is not to turn them into hackers or programmers, but because being engaged in the full range of technology fluencies—including programming—is an educational right of the twenty-first century. This point becomes even more important when over 90% of the youth that come to the Clubhouse have never been in a computer class during their entire K–12 schooling experience. The Computer Clubhouse then becomes an important space for access to computer programming tools and skills.

IMPLICATIONS FOR CREATING DESIGN CULTURES

A simple story of our efforts to seed a programming culture in the Computer Clubhouse would focus on the Scratch software alone. Our results indicate that Scratch indeed was integrated into the portfolio of design activities in this particular Clubhouse, yet the true test of diffusion and integration will come as we are releasing the software to other Clubhouses within the network and beyond. We found that, on their own, Clubhouse youth discovered and used many commands while others hardly were used. These findings are especially surprising given the lack of formal instruction and the fact that the mentors had no prior programming experience. As part of our intervention, Scratch was never intended to be a shrink-wrapped package that was simply handed to members; rather, it was introduced in tandem with other changes at the Computer Clubhouse.

The introduction of both Scratch and undergraduate mentors would not have been possible without a change in relationships at the Clubhouse. A formal partnership was forged between the university and the Clubhouse's community host organization in order to gain support from the organization's infrastructure for these changes. By establishing goals, expectations, and communication protocols with the community organization, we were able to gain crucial buy-in on multiple levels, from the director to the coordinators. Through these various changes, a culture of programming began to emerge more in line with the initial vision of the technology fluency aspect of the Clubhouse learning model.

An equally pressing question is, of course, why did Clubhouse youth choose to get involved in Scratch programming given that they had many other design options? A good answer might have been provided by Caitlin Kelleher and Randy Pausch (2005), who noted how programming can become more accessible for novices "by simplifying the mechanics of programming, by providing support for learners, and by providing students with motivation to learn to program" (p. 131). We think that Scratch addresses all three of these areas. For one, the design of the Scratch blocks simplifies the mechanics of programming by eliminating syntax errors, providing feedback about placement of command blocks, and giving immediate feedback for experiments. Furthermore, we think that the social infrastructure of the Clubhouse is important in providing support for novice programmers. While the mentors did not have any prior programming experiences—all of them were liberal arts majors—they were willing to listen and encourage youth in pursuing their programming projects. Often we could observe youth recruiting mentors to be collaborators or sounding boards for their project ideas. At times, we saw Clubhouse youth teach mentors a few things they had learned about Scratch. While mentors are often associated with being more knowledgeable than their mentees, here we found a more equitable relationship that turned both members and mentors into learners. This need for an audience and resources may also explain the success of the recently opened Scratch Web site (http://www.scratch.mit.edu), which allows programmers to upload their projects and share them with others.

Finally, we think that the multimedia aspect of Scratch facilitated urban youth's engagement in programming. The project archive provided ample evidence that

Clubhouse members were savvy about various media genres and interested in not only using them but also producing their own versions. Many Scratch programs started with images pulled from the Web and centered on popular characters. In fact, we have evidence from other analyses that Scratch projects focused on generic characters were more often abandoned than those that used popular characters. Youth interest in technology starts with digital media and might thus serve as a more promising pathway into programming. The broad spectrum of media designs—from video games to music videos and greeting cards—is a true indicator of youth's interest in not only being users of digital media (as they do on a regular and personal basis) but in going beyond mere consumption to become content creators themselves, a role often denied to urban youth. We argue that youth require technological fluency of how to construct new media in order to become critical consumers and producers. We think that such directions in community technology developments are particularly important for urban youth, who are often seen as pushing new adaptations and transformations of media, but are also perceived as standing on the sidelines of technology development and production.

As illustrated in the examples of Clubhouse work, multiple aspects of media-rich production in informal settings provide youth access to technological fluency that empower them as designers in a setting where their contributions are valued. Our approach to technological fluency in the media-rich Scratch software and in the programming projects in the Clubhouse was grounded in youth practices. Previous discussions have cast this issue mostly in terms of access to digital equipment, talking about the Digital Divide when, in fact, the focus should be on the participation gap that exists in today's society. It is here that our work with Scratch production gathers particular relevance in light of the inequitable access and participation of minority and low-income youth in digital technologies. Technological fluency is not just about knowing how to code, but also involves the personal expression as illustrated in the previous examples. These projects emphasize graphic, music, and video—media that have been found to be at the core of technology interests for youth. Youth needs to be encouraged to become consumers, designers, and inventors with new technologies. Places like the Computer Clubhouse can provide access to creative, critical, and technical media-production skills such as programming in low-income communities and fill a gap not covered elsewhere.

A Place for the Future

Yasmin Kafai, Kylie Peppler, and Robbin Chapman

The goals for this volume were quite ambitious because we wanted to provide a better understanding of the Computer Clubhouse as an idea and as a space for learning. Our choice of words is intentional because "a space for" means that each Computer Clubhouse is precisely designed, despite the fact that this might not be obvious at first glance. From the green table and chairs on rollers to the evaluation efforts, much thought has been put into creating spaces that provide safe haven for creativity and community building—two activities that support each other in beneficial ways. Most important, the "idea" part of the Computer Clubhouse was to create an embodiment of a constructionist learning culture, to bring the idea of learning by designing to fruition. Some may argue this is easier to achieve in informal spaces than in schools, but we hope the chapters in this book provide evidence that much support and, yes, design go into developing and sustaining these efforts.

One way to shine light on the Clubhouse learning model was to select different lenses that would allow us to talk about the Clubhouse members' creative projects. We wanted to showcase the kind of learning that happens in the Clubhouse and is so relevant to youths' intellectual and social development, but is rarely provided in school. Our purpose was to illustrate the kind of design processes and how they address critical twenty-first-century learning skills by fostering creativity, technology fluency, and critical stances in using, designing, and performing with digital media. Our list of the multiple productions that Clubhouse youth are engaged in is by no means exhaustive; we provided glimpses into everyday Clubhouse activities.

We also wanted to give credence to the crucial role of community that the Clubhouse Network exemplifies on multiple levels: in the way that peer expertise is shared within a Clubhouse community, how mentors not only contribute but also learn in Clubhouses, and how intranets, like the Village, foster a sense of global community among the 100+ Clubhouses. This community supported by coordinators, Clubhouse Network geographic liaisons, and community organizations illustrates how design activities can connect youth across the globe.

Finally, each organization needs to undergo continuous processes of self-reflection and engagement to understand its impact and features in need of change. The Clubhouse Network has conducted these self-studies on multiple levels, from examining individual Clubhouse cultures and participation across the network to generating programs that are sensitive to equitable participation, such as the Girls' Day effort.

REFLECTIONS ON THE LEARNING MODEL

Amidst the proliferation of after-school programs and community technology centers, the Clubhouse learning model occupies a unique and much needed niche. Perhaps most important, the Clubhouse learning model emphasizes creativity with digital media. Today, there is much recognition that creativity will drive society's development and growth, but that schools often fail students in this respect, in particular those from underserved communities. By contrast, the Clubhouse Network creates a global community of designers. The Village supports Clubhouse members' interests in media, like the popular networking site, MySpace, and video-sharing site, YouTube. In addition, the Village fosters an exchange and discussion of ideas and design projects across borders.

Finally, the Clubhouse is also part of a larger effort to develop new constructionist technologies. Its close connection to research groups at the MIT Media Lab has provided fertile partnerships. In the chapters of this book, several examples for new technology designs, such as the Pearls of Wisdom, Scratch, or Hook-ups, illustrated that educational technologies can and need to be designed for informal contexts, as most efforts have focused on classrooms and schools. Here, the Clubhouse's departure from traditional after-school programs and community technology centers is most obvious. Given that the Clubhouse culture is dedicated to supporting youth in design of new technology applications, being part of the development process is a natural and fruitful extension.

We might take the features of the Computer Clubhouse learning model for granted now, but at the time when it was founded, many features were new and continue to be unique. The work presented in the book provides counter narratives of technology use and design by disenfranchised youth. It illustrates that it is possible to create a learning culture where technology design and use can be culturally and academically relevant at the same time. Participation in the twenty-first century is more than just knowing how to use technology; it is also about knowing how to design with technology. This is at the core of the Clubhouse learning model.

Still, becoming tech-savvy is not the only goal of the Computer Clubhouse. In fact, many coordinators see preparing youth for leadership in their lives and community as equally valuable goals. Rather than teaching about leadership, Clubhouse projects situate youth in roles allowing them to be in charge of their own learning, developing and realizing their ideas, problem solving and persevering, and recruiting support and feedback. The Clubhouse not only puts members in charge of their own learning, but also places them in charge of teaching others and providing leadership within the Clubhouse community. Thus, the Computer Clubhouse provides a case in point that marginalized youth can be entrusted with sophisticated and expensive equipment, can become designers rather than users of technology, and in the process can develop perspectives for their futures.

ACCESS AND EQUITY

Prior discussions about the Digital Divide have evolved as costs of new technologies have plummeted and recent reports (Lenhart, et al., 2005; Roberts et al., 2005) have documented that access to computing technologies at home has become widespread across the United States, albeit with differing degrees of saturation. In the United States, the attention has shifted from the Digital Divide to the participation gap. The participation gap captures the growing distance between youth who know how to use technology for browsing the Internet and gaming and those who know how to employ technology toward more creative and expressive ends (Jenkins, Clinton, Purushotma, Robinson, & Weigel, 2006; Warschauer, 2004). Having creative and technical skills allows youth to participate in digital culture.

However, the Clubhouse model continues to endure and flourish here in the United States and in other parts of the world where access to technology is not the most pressing issue. What does this mean for our evolving understanding of the Digital Divide or the participation gap? In the United States, the longevity of the model speaks to what's still not available to youth: access to creative technologies in a collaborative learning setting. In part, this is due to the expense of many professional software packages. Fred Riedel, the Computer Clubhouse coordinator in Harlem, New York, has observed that these types of creative learning opportunities do not even exist in elite private schools, but especially not in Internet cafés.

Furthermore, having access to such creative tools, even the Clubhouse community is often not enough to draw youth into design work (Chapman, 2004; Peppler & Kafai, 2008a). As previous chapters demonstrate, the success of the Clubhouse learning model is largely due to the mentors and occasional instructional workshops that support creative production in the Clubhouse Network (Kafai, Desai, et al., 2008; Kafai et al., 2007; Peppler & Kafai, 2008a). Creating spaces supportive of creative work is a challenge shared by schools, after-school communities (such as Boys and Girls Clubs and local libraries), and youth working at home alone (Sefton-Green & Buckingham, 1998), which could all benefit from some of the lessons learned at the Computer Clubhouse for promoting constructionist learning.

FUTURE OF THE COMPUTER CLUBHOUSE NETWORK

As the Clubhouse Network continues to expand in the next decade, there are many plans to move forward and address the changing needs of its members. Several programs are on the cusp of a full-scale rollout, and Network staff have many ideas for the more distant future of the Network. As the vision for the original Computer Clubhouse continues to scale and expand, there are several new and exciting directions in which it could grow, some of which came up in our interviews with Network staff and Clubhouse coordinators featured in Chapter 3 and discussed here.

In general, there is a continuing vision to expand the Clubhouse Network to incorporate new locations across the globe and offer a growing number of youth access to creative design technologies. In order to do so effectively, there are several strategies the Clubhouse Network can envision. First, several of the Network staff discussed that it would be ideal to open new Clubhouses in clusters within a small geographic region. This is for several practical reasons, but would allow youth to communicate with others who speak the same native language, facilitate travel between Clubhouses as well as face-to-face collaboration. As Gail Breslow, the director of the Computer Clubhouse Network states, "Right now, we have these island Clubhouses with none around them. I would like to change that. For example, we have one Clubhouse in Russia. That's a fixed cost, of course, so leveraging that fixed cost (or amortizing it) is important." The Clubhouse Network is now in a crucial point in its development: It's large enough to impact substantial groups of youth across the globe but is small enough to still maintain the close-knit family feel.

At the current time several existing international educational technology programs are interested in folding their programs into the Clubhouse Network. This would present new opportunities for rapid growth, adding hundreds of Clubhouses to the Network at one time. However, as Patricia Díaz from the Clubhouse Network points out,

> We've grown so much in the past 10 years, and if we want to grow in the same way in the next 10 years, an increase in number of Clubhouses would make a big difference in what would happen with the existing model. I think a network of a hundred Clubhouses is still a network where everybody knows everybody; where it's very personal; where a team of 10 people can support the whole network. If we were to grow tenfold, the existing model would have to change because then we're talking about thousands of Clubhouses. At some point, you lose that personal level and a sense of everybody knowing everybody."

Finding new models and ways to support continued collaboration would be an ongoing challenge in cases such as this, perhaps placing central the role of the Clubhouse Village site as well as smaller regional meetings.

As the Clubhouse continues to grow, Network staff is committed to continuing connections with Clubhouse alumni to create a vast social network of past and current members. Currently, there are several initiatives to connect alumni through existing social networking sites. And what Brenda Abanavas would like to see more of in the future is "an almost natural turnover so that the young people who grow up in the Clubhouse are in some way still a vital part of the Clubhouse Network. That can either take the form of some of them coming back as Clubhouse coordinators, which we certainly have had, but also by being involved in whatever capacity that they are able to give back. They could create internships for young members, be guest speakers, or return as a volunteer." In this way, new connections can be forged between past and present members.

One of the other hopes for the Network, as network staff Jeff Arthur says, is to become "a household name where you entrust your kids, where colleges can look at Clubhouse on somebody's application, and say, 'Oh, you went to a Computer Clubhouse. You're in!'" By having alumni return to help guide the newest generation of members and by increasing the renown of the network, the hope would be that the Clubhouse could increase the impact that it has on opening doors for the future of its youth.

In addition to thinking about greater involvement of alumni in growing the capacity of current Clubhouse, several of the Clubhouse coordinators have been thinking about how to service a wider range of community members, such as parents, schools, and other adults in the community. As Clubhouse coordinator Almetris Stanley relays, "I really see working with more schools in the community and the Clubhouse being a field trip destination. I could imagine having the Clubhouse experience on wheels. Everybody can't fit in here but we could come to you and we could do some innovative Clubhouse activities at your site. I see us growing to serve more kids, being a resource for the schools and other community-based organizations as well." By doing so, individual Clubhouse sites could increase the scope of services offered to the community, widening the impact of and exposure to the Clubhouse learning model.

As members become more advanced, some of the Clubhouses have begun to think about tying the Clubhouse to other academic instruction to prepare youth to enter math, science, and engineering fields. As Clubhouse coordinator Luversa Sullivan observes,

> What has happened here at our Clubhouse is that members don't leave. So at some point, making Flash animations and movies, audio, and even Scratch gets to be kind of the old tool. They become so fluent with it that they have to start using those tools in different ways. What we've done is we have expanded the Clubhouse program into what we call our Clever Program, which is for advanced students who are interested in math, science, and engineering. They go on to the Clever Program and they use different tools to help teach the entire Clubhouse community.

All of the aforementioned directions indicate a vital future for the Clubhouse Network as it expands in new ways. While there is surely room for more Computer Clubhouses, other options might be to promote the introduction of "Clubhouse-like ideas," as Network director Gail Breslow calls them, "to others, whether it's schools with extended-day programs or community technology centers that might not have the resources or the wherewithal to start full Clubhouses." She brings up the example of Colombia, which, as a country, has invested in setting up "mini Internet sites that are not being really well utilized. They're not Clubhouses, but there are ways to have little Clubhouse activities going on in there and can we help either by consulting to governments or consulting to Ministries of Education." The coming years will show in which directions these ideas will take off, in particular with the growing interest in after-school programs and recognition of their benefits for youth development.

CLUBHOUSE MEMBERS ARE THE FUTURE

We want to close this book in the way we started it—with the Clubhouse members—who are not only the reason that Clubhouses were started but also the driving forces in them. Their successes are the most important outcome measure of the Computer Clubhouse. What is most evident are the enduring lessons, related to work, education, and life, that members take from their Clubhouse experiences. When members, both past and present, speak of their futures they all find connections between Clubhouse activities and relationships and their own personal successes. These young women and young men are bringing their Clubhouse lessons into their futures.

> If not for the Computer Clubhouse, I would not have gone to college. I was confused about what I wanted and unaware of the opportunities. Clubhouse staff and mentors opened my eyes to career options with art, sparked my interest in learning, and gave me direction.
>
> —Guillermo, age 21

> The most valuable thing I've learned at the Clubhouse is to create myself. The Clubhouse really showed me what I was capable of doing and helped me get started. Now I want to be an engineer because I'm able to design things in my own unique way, with my own ideas. The Clubhouse made me unafraid to make mistakes and try new things.
>
> —Amy, age 22

> My people skills have grown. A lot of communication and interaction takes place at the Clubhouse. Developing good communication skills is important for survival. Being involved in the Clubhouse, I had to develop them, if I was going to teach and mentor others. I have a better understanding of how to get schoolwork done. I need to stay focused, reach for my goals, and give my best in all that I do.
>
> —Mike, age 18

> I decided to become a Clubhouse mentor because I felt that I could be a part of the development and improvement of it in the next years. I was a member for years and I know how important the Clubhouse is. It is important to be a Clubhouse mentor because in a sense you are aiding the youth who could be doing nothing with developing skills that could help them in life.
>
> —Tammy, age 19

Whether as members, mentors, coordinators, or whatever paths youth have decided to pursue, the adage known to every member still holds true: "Once a member, always a member." This promise—perhaps the most important of all—is extended to all who enter a Computer Clubhouse.

References

Anthes, G. (2008, July 10). The new face of R&D: What's cooking at IBM, HP, and Microsoft [Electronic version]. *Computerworld*. Retrieved September 30, 2008, from http://www.computerworld.com/action/article.do?command=viewArticleBasic&articleId=9108098&pageNumber=1.

Beamish, A. (1999). Approaches to community computing: Bringing technology to low-income groups. In D. A. Schön, B. Sanyal, & W. J. Mitchell (Eds.), *High technology and low-income communities: Prospects for the positive use of advanced information technology* (pp. 349–368). Cambridge, MA: MIT Press.

Bennett, A. (1999). Subcultures or neo-tribes? Rethinking the relationship between youth, style, and musical taste. *Sociology, 33*(3), 599–617.

Bers, M. U. (2008). Civic identities, online technologies: From designing civic curriculum to supporting civic experiences. In W. L. Bennett (Ed.), *Civic life online: Learning how digital media can engage youth* (pp. 139–160). Cambridge, MA: MIT Press.

Brown, A. L. (1994). The advancement of learning. *Educational Researcher, 23*(8), 4–12.

Bruner, J. (1996). *The culture of education*. Cambridge, MA: Harvard University Press.

Buckingham, D. (2003). *Media education: Literacy, learning, and contemporary culture*. Cambridge, UK: Polity Press.

Cervone, B. (2002). *Taking democracy in hand: Youth action for education change in the San Francisco Bay Area*. Providence, RI: What Kids Can Do & the Forum for Youth Investment.

Chapman, R. (2001). *Redefining equity: Meaningful uses of technology in learning environments*. Paper presented at the IEEE International Conference on Advanced Learning Technologies (ICALT 2001), Madison, WI.

Chapman, R. (2004). Pearls of Wisdom: Social capital building in informal learning environments. In M. Huysman & V. Wulf (Eds.), *Social capital and information technology* (pp. 301–332). Cambridge, MA: MIT Press.

Chapman, R. (2006). *Pearls of Wisdom: Technology for intentional reflection and learning in constructionist cooperatives*. Unpublished doctoral dissertation, Massachusetts Institute of Technology, Cambridge, MA.

Chapman, R. (2007). The reflective mentor model: Growing communities of practice for teacher development in informal learning environments. In C. Kimble and P. Hildreth (Eds.), *Communities of practice: creating learning environments for educators* (pp. 39–64). Charlotte, NC: Information Age Publishing.

Cohen, E. G. (1994). Restructuring the classroom: Conditions for productive small groups. *Review of Educational Research, 64*, 1–35.

Cole, M. (2006). *The fifth dimension*. New York: Russell Sage Foundation Press.

Corbett, C., & St. Rose, A. (2008). *Where the girls are: The facts about gender equity in education*. Washington, DC: Educational Foundation of the American Association of University Women.

Dawkins, R. (1976/1999). *The selfish gene*. Oxford University Press.

Degenne, A., & Forse, M. (1999). *Introducing social networks*. Thousand Oaks, CA: Sage.

Díaz, P. (2003). The Computer Clubhouse Village: A virtual meeting place for an emerging community of learners. In J.V. Carrasquero, F. Welsch, C. Urrea, & C.-D. Tso (Eds.), *Politics and Information Systems: Technologies and Applications* (pp. 47–50) (Post-conference ed.). Orlando, FL: International Institute of Informatics and Systemics.

DuBois, D. L., & Karcher, M. J. (2005). Youth mentoring: theory, research, and practice. In D. L. DuBois & M. J. Karcher (Eds.), *Handbook of youth mentoring* (pp. 2–12). Thousand Oaks, CA: Sage.

Eisenberg, M. (2003). Mindstuff: Educational technology beyond the computer. *Convergence, 9*(2), 29–53.

Erkut, S., & Marx, F. (2005). *Hear our voices: Girls and technology at the computer clubhouse.* (Final Report). Wellesley, MA: Wellesley Centers for Research on Women.

Florida, R. (2002). *The rise of the creative class*. New York: Basic Books.

Gallagher, L., & Michalchik, V. (2007, July). *Assessing youth impact of the Computer Clubhouse Network: May 2007 Youth Impact Survey Administration*. Menlo Park, CA: SRI International. Retrieved December 17, 2008, from http://www.computerclubhouse.org/evaluation/Clubhouse%20Survey-May%202007.pdf

Gallagher, L., Michalchik, V., & Emery, D. (2006). *Assessing youth impact of the Computer Clubhouse Network: May 2006 Youth Impact Survey Administration*. Palo Alto, CA: SRI International.

Goode, J. (2004). *Mind the gap: The digital dimension of college access.* Unpublished dissertation, University of California at Los Angeles.

Guzdial, M. (2004). Programming environments for novices. In S. Fincher & M. Petre (Eds.), *Computer science education research* (pp. 127–154). Lisse, the Netherlands: Taylor & Francis.

Hart, S. (2006). Breaking literacy boundaries through critical service-learning: Education for the silenced and marginalized. *Mentoring and Tutoring, 14*(1), 17–32.

Hirsch, B. J. (2005). *A place to call home: After-school programs for urban youth*. Washington, DC: American Psychological Association.

Hirsch, B. J., & Wong, V. (2005). After-school programs. In D. L. DuBois & M. J. Karcher (Eds.), *Handbook of youth mentoring* (pp. 14–29). Thousand Oaks, CA: Sage.

Holt, J. (1977). On alternative schools. *Growing Without Schooling, 17*, 5–6.

Howard, R. W. (2006). Bending towards justice: service learning and social capital as means to the tipping point. *Mentoring and Tutoring, 14*(1), 5–15.

Jacobi, M. (1991). Mentoring and undergraduate success: a literature review. *Review of Educational Research, 61*(4), 505–532.

Jenkins, H., Clinton, K., Purushotma, R., Robinson, A. J., & Weigel, M. (2006). *Confronting the challenges of participatory culture: Media education for the 21st century*. Chicago: MacArthur Foundation.

Kafai, Y. B. (2006). Constructionism. In K. Sawyer (Ed.), *Cambridge handbook of the learning sciences* (pp. 35–46). New York: Cambridge University Press.

Kafai, Y. B., Desai, S., Peppler, K., Chiu, G., & Moya, J. (2008). Mentoring partnerships in a community technology center: A constructionist approach for fostering equitable service learning. *Mentoring & Tutoring, 16*(2), 191–205.

Kafai, Y. B., & Peppler, K. (2008). Learning from krumping: Collective agency in dance performance cultures. In *Proceedings of the eighth International Conference of the Learning Sciences* (pp. 430–437). N.p.: International Society of the Learning Sciences; distributed Lulu.com.

Kafai, Y. B., Peppler, K., Alavez, M., & Ruvalcaba, O. (2006). Seeds of a computer culture: An archival analysis of programming artifacts from a community technology center.

In S. A. Barab, K. E. Hay, & D. T. Hickey (Eds.), *Proceedings of the seventh international conference of the learning sciences* (pp. 942–943). Mahwah, NJ: Erlbaum.

Kafai, Y. B., Peppler, K., & Chiu, G. (2007). High tech programmers in low-income communities: Seeding reform in a community technology center. In C. Steinfeld, B. T. Pentland, M. Ackerman, & N. Contractor (Eds.), *Communities and technologies: Proceedings of the third communities and technologies conference.* London: Springer.

Kafai, Y. B., & Resnick, M. (1996). Constructionism in practice: Designing, thinking, and learning in a digital world. Mahwah, NJ: Erlbaum.

Kelleher, C., & Pausch, R. (2005). Lowering the barriers to programming: A taxonomy of programming environments and languages for novice programmers. *ACM Computing Surveys, 37(2),* 88–137.

Kirshner, B. (2007). Introduction: Youth activism as a context for learning and development. *American Behavioral Scientist, 51(3),* 367–379.

Kozol, J. (1991). Savage inequalities: Children in America's schools. New York: Harper Collins.

Kremer, G. (1991). *George Washington Carver: In his own words.* Columbia: University of Missouri Press.

LaChappelle, D. (Producer/Director). (2005). *Rize* [Motion picture]. United States: Lions Gate Home Entertainment.

Lave, J., & Wenger, E. (1991). *Situated learning: Legitimate peripheral participation.* Cambridge: Cambridge University Press.

Lenhart, A., Madden, M., & Hitlin, P. (2005). *Teens and technology: Youth are leading the transition to a fully wired and mobile nation.* (Pew Internet report). Retrieved August 8, 2008, from http://www.pewInternet.org/report_display.asp?r=-162

Lenhart, A., Madden, M., Macgill, A.R., & Smith, A. (2007). *Teen content creators.* (Pew Internet & American Life Project). Retrieved January 3, 2009, from http://www.pewresearch.org/pubs/670/teen-content-creators

Leventhal, T., & Brooks-Gunn, J. (2003). Children and youth in neighborhood contexts. *Current Directions in Psychological Science, 12(1),* 27–31.

Maeda, J. (2004). *Creative code.* New York: Thames & Hudson.

Maloney, J., Burd, L., Kafai, Y., Rusk, N., Silverman, B., & Resnick, M. (2004, January). *Scratch: A sneak preview.* Paper presented at the Second International Conference on Creating, Connecting, and Collaborating Through Computing, Kyoto, Japan. Retrieved August 12, 2008, from http://llk.media.mit.edu/projects/scratch/Scratch-SneakPreview.pdf

Maloney, J., Peppler, K., Kafai, Y., Resnick, M., & Rusk, N. (2008, March). *Programming by choice. Urban youth learning programming with Scratch.* Paper presented at the SIGCSE 2008 Conference, Portland, OR.

Margolis, J. (2008). *Towards the shallow end: Education, race, and computers.* Cambridge, MA: MIT Press.

Margolis, J., & Fisher, A. (2003). *Unlocking the clubhouse: Women in computing.* Cambridge, MA: MIT Press.

Michalchik, V., Llorente, C., & Lundh, P. (2008, July). *A place to be your best: Youth outcomes in the Computer Clubhouse.* Menlo Park, CA: SRI International. Retrieved July 25, 2008, from http://www.computerclubhouse.org/evaluation/PlaceToBeYourBest.pdf

Mitchell, W. J., Inouye, A. S., & Blumenthal, M. S. (2003). *Beyond productivity: Information, technology, innovation and creativity.* Washington, DC: National Academies Press.

Monaghan, J., & Lunt, N. (1992). Mentoring: Person, process, practice, and problems. *British Journal of Educational Studies, 40(3),* 248–263.

Monroy-Hernández, A., & Resnick, M. (2008). Empowering kids to create and share programmable media. *Interactions, 15(2),* 50–53.

Papert, S. (1980). *Mindstorms: Children, computers, and powerful ideas.* New York: Basic Books.

Papert, S. (1991). Situating constructionism. In I. Harel & S. Papert (Eds.), *Constructionism* (pp. 1–14). Hillsdale, NJ: Erlbaum.

Papert, S. (1993a). *The children's machine.* New York: Basic Books.

Papert, S. (1993b). *Mindstorms* (2nd ed.). New York: Basic Books.

Papert, S., & Turkle, S. (1992). Epistemological pluralism and the revaluation of the concrete. *Journal of Mathematical Behavior, 11*(1), 3–33.

Pasnik, S., & Meade, T. (2003, November). *Creating in the Clubhouse: Tools for conversations and portfolio development.* New York: Center for Children and Technology. Retrieved July 15, 2008, from: http://cct.edc.org/admin/publications/administrator/Clubhouse_Toolkit.pdf

Peppler, K. (2007). *Creative bytes: Literacy and learning in the media arts practices of urban youth.* Unpublished doctoral dissertation, University of California, Los Angeles.

Peppler, K., & Kafai, Y. B. (2006). Creative codings: Investigating cultural, personal, and epistemological connections in media arts programming. *Proceedings of the seventh international conference of the learning sciences* (pp. 972–973). Mahwah, NJ: Erlbaum.

Peppler, K., & Kafai, Y. B. (2007). From SuperGoo to Scratch: Exploring creative digital media production in informal learning. *Learning, Media, and Technology, 32*(2), 149–166.

Peppler, K., & Kafai, Y. B. (2008a). Developing a design culture in a Computer Clubhouse: The role of local practices and mediators. In *Proceedings of the Eighth International Conference of the Learning Sciences* (pp. 196–203). N.p.: Internaional Society of the Learning Sciences; distributed by Lulu.com.

Perkins, D. N. (1986). *Knowledge as design.* Hillsdale, NJ: Erlbaum.

Pestalozzi, J. H. (1894). How Gertrude teaches her children: An attempt to help mothers to teach their own children and an account of the method. London: The Society of the Friends of Education, Burgdorf.

Pink, D. (2006). *A whole new mind: Why right-brainers will rule the future.* New York, NY: Riverhead Books.

Pryor, T., McMillan, K. C., Lutz, S., & John, K. (2001, October). *Evaluation of the Intel Computer Clubhouse Network, Year 1.* New York: Center for Children and Technology. Retrieved on July 15, 2008 at http://cct.edc.org/admin/publications/report/10_2001b.pdf

Resnick, M. (1996). Towards a practice of "constructional design." In L. Shauble & R. Glaser (Eds.), *Innovations in learning: New environments for education* (pp. 161–174). Hillsdale, NJ: Erlbaum.

Resnick, M. (2006). Computer as paintbrush: Technology, play, and the creative society. In D. Singer, R. Golikoff, & K. Hirsh-Pasek (Eds.), *Play = learning: How play motivates and enhances children's cognitive and social-emotional growth.* Oxford: Oxford University Press.

Resnick, M., Kafai, Y., & Maeda, J. (2003). *A networked, media-rich programming environment to ehance technological fluency at after-school centers in economically disadvantaged communities.* Proposal funded by National Science Foundation (Information Technology Research). Retrieved January 3, 2009, from http://web.media.mit.edu/~mres/papers/scratch-proposal.pdf

Resnick, M., & Rusk, N. (1996). The Computer Clubhouse: Preparing for life in a digital world. *IBM Systems Journal, 35,* 431–440.

Resnick, M., Rusk, N., & Cooke, S. (1999). The Computer Clubhouse: Technological fluency in the inner city. In D. A. Schön, B. Sanyal, & W. J. Mitchell (Eds.), *High technology and low-income communities: Prospects for the positive use of advanced information technology* (pp. 263–285). Cambridge, MA: MIT Press.

Roberts, A. (2000). Mentoring revisited: A phenomenological reading of the literature. *Mentoring and Tutoring, 8*(2), 145–170.

Roberts, D. F., Foehr, U. G., & Rideout, V., (2005). *Generation M: Media in the lives of 8–18 year-olds*. Menlo Park, CA: Kaiser Family Foundation.

Sampson, Z. (2007, February 23). Virginia schools may lose funding [Electronic version]. *The Washington Times*. Retrieved September 30, 2008, from http://www.washingtontimes.com/news/2007/feb/22/20070222-110136-9807r/

Schön, D. A. (1983). *The reflective practitioner: How professionals think in action*. New York, NY: Basic Books.

Schön, D. A. (1987). *Educating the reflective practitioner: Toward a new design for teaching and learning in the professions*. San Francisco: Jossey-Bass.

Sefton-Green, J., & Buckingham, D. (1998). Digital visions: Children's 'creative' uses of multimedia technologies. In J. Sefton-Green (Ed.), *Digital diversions: Youth culture in the age of multimedia* (pp. 62–83). London: UCL Press.

Servon, L. J., & Nelson, M. K. (2002). Urban technology gap. *International Journal of Urban and Regional Research, 22*(2), 419–426.

Sherman, R. (2002). Building young people's lives: One foundation's strategy. *New Direction for Youth Development, 96*, 65–82.

Sullivan, A. (1996). From mentor to muse: Recasting the role of women in relationship with urban adolescent girls. In B. J. Ross Leadbeater & N. Way (Eds.), *Urban girls* (pp. 226–249). New York: NYU Press.

Sutton, R. E. (1991). Equity and computers. *Review of Educational Research, 61*(4), 474–505.

Sylvan, E. (2007). *The sharing of wonderful ideas: Influence and interaction in online communities of creators*. Unpublished dissertation, Massachusetts Institute of Technology, Cambridge, MA.

Turkle, S. & Papert, S. (1990). Epistemological pluralism: Styles and voices within the computer culture. *Signs, 16*(1), 128–157.

Villalpando, O., & Solorzano, D. G. (2005). The role of culture in college preparation programs: A review of the research literature. In W. Tierney, Z. Corwin, & J. Colyar (Eds.), *Preparing for college: Nine elements of effective outreach* (pp. 13–28). Albany: State University of New York Press.

Vogelsang, L. J., & Astin, A. W. (2000). Comparing the effects of community service and service learning. *Michigan Journal of Community Service Learning, 3*, 25–34.

Warschauer, M. (2004). *Technology and social inclusion: Rethinking the digital divide*. Cambridge, MA: MIT Press.

Zagal, J., & Bruckman, A. (2005). From Samba Schools to Computer Clubhouses: Cultural institutions as learning environments. *Convergence, 11*(1), 88–105.

Zhao, Y., Mishra, P., & Girod, M. (2000). A clubhouse is a clubhouse is a clubhouse. *Computers in Human Behavior, 16*, 287–300.

About the Contributors

Brenda Abanavas has over 22 years experience in school-age programming, implementing arts-based programs, and providing case management services to Boston's youth and families. She provides technical training and organizational support to the Intel Computer Clubhouse Network at the Flagship Clubhouse and designs activities for increasing girls' fluency with technology. Brenda is also a geographic liaison for Clubhouses in Europe and the Middle East, as well as the southeastern United States. She works closely with the ICCN director to oversee assessment and evaluation for the network.

Gail Breslow has overseen the dissemination of the Computer Clubhouse to community-based organizations worldwide since 1995. Under her leadership the Clubhouse program has grown from a single location in Boston to over 100 Clubhouses in 21 countries. She also has developed initiatives such as Hear Our Voices (a program for young women); Clubhouse-to-College/Clubhouse-to-Career; and Beyond Four Walls: The Clubhouse as Invention Studio. Previously, Gail spent 12 years as a management consultant with Gemini Consulting, and 3 years as a program director at the American Association for the Advancement of Science. Gail holds an MBA from Stanford University and an undergraduate degree from Oberlin College.

Robbin Chapman earned her Ph.D. and S.M. in electrical engineering and computer science from Massachusetts Institute of Technology. Her research is situated at the intersection of technology, learning, and community, and focuses on engaging learners in critical reflection and other deep learning activities. As a member of Mitchel Resnick's Lifelong Kindergarten group, she developed computational tools and pedagogies for construction and sharing of reflective artifacts within the context of design-based activities. Robbin's publications include several book chapters and various other papers. Her company, Learning Griot, works with clients to develop strategies, workshops, and research for leveraging learning technologies and designing innovative learning environments.

Grace Chiu is a doctoral candidate in urban schooling at the UCLA Graduate School of Education and Information Studies. She is a former public school teacher, professional developer, and community technology center developer. Her dissertation examines peer support networks among urban youth in community technology centers. Grace holds a bachelor's degree from the University of California–Irvine and a master's degree in education from the Harvard Graduate School of Education.

Stina Cooke was a founding staff member of the Computer Clubhouse at the Computer Museum in Boston and later Program Developer for the Intel Computer Clubhouse Network at the Museum of Science in Boston. This program won the 1997 Peter F. Drucker Award for Non-Profit Innovation. In 2005 the 100th Computer Clubhouse was opened around the world. Currently Stina is designing and building virtual exhibits in Second Life with the Exploratorium in San Francisco and the Tech Museum of Innovation in San Jose, California.

Shiv Desai is a doctoral student in urban schooling at the UCLA Graduate School of Education and Information Studies. He is also an English teacher at Opportunities Unlimited Charter High School for 9th–12th graders. He infuses critical race theory, critical theory, and anticolonialism theory into the curriculum. His dissertation investigates how high school students utilize spoken word poetry to critically analyze their world.

Patricia Díaz is the knowledge manager for the Intel Computer Clubhouse Network based at the Museum of Science in Boston. She devises and implements strategies for knowledge sharing among more than 100 Clubhouses in 21 countries around the world including the redesign and use of the Village intranet site in collaboration with colleagues at the MIT Media Lab. As geographic liaison to Latin America, Patricia supports the Clubhouses in Argentina, Brazil, Colombia, Costa Rica, Mexico, and Panama. Patricia has a B.A. in cognitive science and music from Wellesley College and an M.Ed. in Technology, Innovation and Education from the Harvard Graduate School of Education

Yasmin Kafai is a professor of learning sciences at the Graduate School of Education at the University of Pennsylvania. Her research focuses on the cultural, social, and creative learning experiences of youth as designers of games, simulations, and virtual worlds. She has published and edited several books: *Beyond Barbie and Mortal Kombat: New Perspectives on Gender and Gaming; Constructionism in Practice: Learning and Designing in a Digital World;* and *Minds in Play: Computer Game Design as a Context for Children's Learning.* She earned a DEUG from the Université de Haute Bretagne, a diplom in psychology from the Technical University of Berlin and a doctorate in education from Harvard University.

John Maloney is the lead programmer for Scratch, a new programmable toolkit that lets kids create and share their own games, animated stories, and interactive art. Prior to joining the Lifelong Kindergarten group, John worked for computer pioneer Alan Kay, under whom he developed key parts of Squeak, an experimental programming system for elementary school children. He also worked at Walt Disney Imagineering, where he built an experimental handheld electronic guide for theme park guests. Prior to working at Disney, John worked at Apple, Sun Microsystems Labs, and Xerox. John has a Ph.D. in computer science from the University of Washington and M. S. and B. S. degrees in electrical engineering and computer science from MIT.

Amon Millner is a doctoral candidate in the MIT Media Lab's Lifelong Kindergarten group. He develops tools, activities, and spaces for youth to create physical interactions with computer-based objects. He leads the efforts to connect the Scratch programming language to the physical world and helped design the Scratch Sensor Board. As a part of his Hook-ups research project, members at several Computer Clubhouses have invented unique physical computer interfaces using sensor boards. Amon has mentored and/or been an active member in Clubhouses and other after-school community technology centers since 2000. He holds degrees from USC, Georgia Tech, and MIT.

Jesse Moya is a former teacher and director of youth outreach programs and a current doctoral student and researcher at UCLA's Graduate School of Education. His research interests include understanding and improving the educational experiences of urban school students, with a particular focus on culturally relevant and critical pedagogies, the Latino high school student experience, and quality access to high-status technology learning opportunities.

Kylie Peppler is an assistant professor of learning sciences at Indiana University–Bloomington. Her research focuses on literacy and learning in the context of the arts and new technologies. Her work on the media arts practices of Computer Clubhouse youth received a Spencer Foundation dissertation fellowship and was extended with a UC Presidential Postdoctoral Fellowship in 2007. Peppler's background is grounded in the arts as a sculptor of new media. She earned a B.A. in psychology and French from Indiana University, as well as a Ph.D. in education from the University of California–Los Angeles.

Mitchel Resnick is Professor of Learning Research at the MIT Media Lab and cofounder of the Computer Clubhouse project. His research focuses on the development of new technologies and activities to engage people in creative learning experiences. His Lifelong Kindergarten research group developed the "programmable bricks" that were the basis for the LEGO MindStorms and PicoCricket construction kits. The group recently developed a new programming language, called Scratch, which makes it easier for kids to create interactive stories, games, and animations, as well as and share their creations on the Web. Resnick earned a B.S. in physics from Princeton, and an M.S. and Ph.D. in computer science from MIT.

Natalie Rusk is a cofounder of the Computer Clubhouse. She initiated the program while working as Director of Education at the Computer Museum. She has more than 15 years experience developing and directing creative technology programs for youth in museums and after-school centers. She has served as project director of the PIE Network and other NSF-funded collaborative initiatives. She is a research specialist in the Lifelong Kindergarten group at the MIT Media Lab, contributing to the design of Scratch programming language and other new technologies. She is currently pursuing doctoral studies at Tufts University, investigating creative approaches to supporting children's positive emotional development.

Elisabeth Sylvan is project director of the Kids' Survey Network at TERC. Her research focuses on building tools and environments that support social design activities and studying learning communities from a network perspective. For her thesis she developed a model of how learners collaborate by studying their communication and idea exchange in Online Communities of Creators (OCOCs), including the Computer Clubhouse Village. She received a M.S. and Ph.D. in Media Arts and Sciences from MIT and a B.S. in Psychology from Carnegie Mellon University.

Index